The Degrowth Alternative

Degrowth is a planned economic contraction in wealthy countries that reduces production and consumption—and, by extension, greenhouse gas emissions and stresses on global ecosystems—to sustainable levels within ecological limits. This book explores the idea of degrowth as an economic alternative to offer a more sustainable and just future.

A growing number of scientists and scholars now recognize that a system that continues to prioritize economic growth will prevent us from effectively addressing the dual environmental crises of climate change and biodiversity loss. To establish the case for degrowth, the text opens by posing critical questions about our current system and identifying its limitations, as well as discussing the ineffectiveness of "false solutions" that seem to offer something new but would actually preserve the status quo. The concept of degrowth is then fully introduced along with a discussion of core principles and goals as well as major critiques and questions. The book explores what living in a degrowth society would entail and the policies needed to support degrowth. Finally, the work concludes by examining the opportunities and challenges for degrowth and a successful transition to a sustainable steady-state economy.

This book provides an advanced introduction to the environmental issues around degrowth for students, scholars and activists interested in economic alternatives, sustainability and the environment.

Diana Stuart is an Associate Professor in the Sustainable Communities Program and in the School of Earth and Sustainability at Northern Arizona University, USA.

Ryan Gunderson is an Assistant Professor of Sociology and Social Justice Studies in the Department of Sociology and Gerontology and Affiliate of the Institute for the Environment and Sustainability at Miami University, USA.

Brian Petersen is an Associate Professor in the Geography, Planning and Recreation Department at Northern Arizona University, USA.

Routledge Studies in Ecological Economics

For more information about this series, please visit: www.routledge.com/series/RSEE

The Degrowth Alternative

A Path to Address our
Environmental Crisis?

**Diana Stuart, Ryan Gunderson and
Brian Petersen**

Routledge
Taylor & Francis Group

LONDON AND NEW YORK

First published 2021
by Routledge
2 Park Square, Milton Park, Abingdon, Oxon OX14 4RN

and by Routledge
52 Vanderbilt Avenue, New York, NY 10017

Routledge is an imprint of the Taylor & Francis Group, an informa business

© 2021 Diana Stuart, Ryan Gunderson and Brian Petersen

The right of Diana Stuart, Ryan Gunderson and Brian Petersen to
be identified as authors of this work has been asserted by them in
accordance with sections 77 and 78 of the Copyright, Designs and
Patents Act 1988.

British Library Cataloguing-in-Publication Data
A catalogue record for this book is available from the British Library

Library of Congress Cataloging-in-Publication Data
A catalog record has been requested for this book

ISBN: 978-0-367-89466-5 (hbk)
ISBN: 978-1-003-01930-5 (ebk)

Typeset in Times New Roman
by codeMantra

Contents

1 Addressing our environmental crisis

The words "crisis" and "emergency" are increasingly used by scientists and in the media to describe the state of our environment. For example, in 2019 an article representing the views of 11,000 scientists was published in *BioScience*, titled "World Scientists' Warning of a Climate Emergency" (Ripple et al. 2019). Also, in 2019, the "Call it a Climate Crisis" campaign urged media organizations to use the words "climate crisis" instead of "climate change," resulting in a widespread increase in the use of the term.

The terms "ecological crisis" and "biodiversity crisis" are also now commonly used by conservation scientists and in the media. For example, a letter representing almost 100 scientists was published in October of 2018 titled: "Facts about our ecological crisis are incontrovertible" (Green et al. 2018). A year later, a "bleak" United Nations report on biodiversity and ecosystem services (IPBES 2019a) resulted in scientists publicly calling for rapid funding and intervention to address the "biodiversity crisis" (Malcom et al. 2019).

Are we indeed facing multiple environmental crises? General definitions of a "crisis" include a decisive moment or crucial time, a critical phase that determines all future events, a condition of danger or precarity, threats to primary goals, being affected by serious problems, extreme trouble, and a time of great difficulty. In addition, according to Venette (2003: 43), a "crisis is a process of transformation where the old system can no longer be maintained." Evidence suggests that, in terms of all of these different meanings, we are in a state of environmental crisis, which includes the dual crises of climate change and biodiversity loss. We briefly present some of the most recent and compelling scientific evidence demonstrating the reality and severity of these crises below.

Our presentation of the evidence of these crises is brief, as the overall objective of this book is to examine how we can best address them. We present some of the most authoritative and boldest statements from scientists about the possible and likely impacts if we stay on our current course. Then we quickly shift to focus on solutions. For reasons we will describe, we are skeptical of popularly proposed solutions to tackle these crises and instead seek out more far-reaching and transformative alternatives. We focus on a key lever in our system that drives the speed and direction of our material and energy flows, economic growth, and examine degrowth as an alternative to move us towards a better and more sustainable future.

Evidence of our climate and biodiversity crises

Mounting evidence indicates that we are in a climate crisis. With only a little more than 1°C increase in average global temperatures since preindustrial levels, we are already seeing serious impacts including unprecedented fires, floods, and hurricanes; and much more severe impacts are projected as warming continues. Steffen et al. (2018) explain the real possibility of reaching a critical threshold of warming or a global tipping point after which additional warming would be uncontrollable, resulting in a "Hothouse Earth" scenario. In *Nature*, Lenton et al. (2019: 595) state that climate change "is an existential threat to civilization," explaining that "the evidence from tipping points alone suggests that we are in a state of planetary emergency: both the risk and urgency of the situation are acute."

Climate impacts are already unfolding and the crisis will amplify with increasing climate-related disasters, melting ice, and rising sea levels. The 2018 Intergovernmental Panel on Climate Change (IPCC) Special Report *Global Warming of 1.5°C* contains much bolder language than previous reports to stress the significant difference in impacts between a 1.5°C and a 2°C increase in average global temperatures and the need for immediate, unprecedented, and far-reaching action. In addition, a 2019 report in the *Lancet* details how climate change is already impacting human health globally and warns of devastating health impacts as warming continues (Watts et al. 2019). Lastly, Ripple et al. (2019: 1), representing the Alliance of World Scientists, identify "disturbing" and "worrisome" vital signs of climate impacts that they state "clearly and unequivocally" illustrates we are in a "climate emergency."

Although the climate crisis contributes to biodiversity loss (Thomas et al. 2004), it is considered a separate, yet related, crisis. Conservation biologists pointed out years ago that we are in the midst of the sixth global mass extinction event, driven by humans (Barnosky et al. 2011), also referred to as the "extinction tsunami" (Lovejoy 2017) or "biological annihilation" (Ceballos et al. 2017). Recent indicators of a biodiversity crisis include half of all vertebrate populations in decline (Ceballos et al. 2017), a global extinction rate of approximately 200 species each day (Green et al. 2018), the loss of 29% of birds in North America since 1970 (Rosenberg et al. 2019), and 1 million species (25%) facing extinction globally (IPBES 2019a). A comprehensive report from the Intergovernmental Science-Policy Platform on Biodiversity and Ecosystem Services (IPBES 2019a) concludes that humans are driving global changes in plant and animal life that are unprecedented in history.

The biodiversity crisis will increasingly impact human societies. While many people overlook human dependency on other species, scientists continue to argue that at current rates we will alter the natural world in ways that threaten not only human well-being but also human existence (Ceballos et al. 2015). The concept of ecosystem services has been used for decades to emphasize the ways that humans benefit from and depend on ecosystems (Millennium Ecosystem Assessment 2005) and projections of global change reveal the potential severity of social impacts from biodiversity loss. The IPBES media release (2019b) states that species loss has accelerated to rates that "constitutes a direct threat to human well-being in all regions of the world." The United Nations biodiversity chief warns of ecological thresholds and tipping points that could result in a cascade of extinctions, collapse, and social impacts (Conley 2019).

If a crisis is a decisive moment, crucial time, or a critical phase that determines future events, then, according to scientists, we are in a state of environmental crisis. If a crisis is a condition of danger or precarity that poses serious problems, extreme trouble, and great difficulty, then the science again indicates we are in a climate and ecological crisis. In addition to scientists, an increasing number of other people now recognize these serious threats. For example, United States (US) public opinion polls reveal that more than a quarter of Americans consider climate change a "crisis" with a further 36% defining it as a "serious problem" (CBS News 2019). In addition, 60% of Americans polled think government should do something to address global warming and 70% believe environmental protection is more important than economic growth (Marlon et al. 2019). In the United Kingdom (UK), 85% of citizens are concerned about climate change, 52% are very concerned, and 55% think the UK should bring emissions to net zero before 2050 targets (Dickman and Skinner 2019).

If we define a crisis as "a process of transformation where the old system can no longer be maintained" (Venette 2003: 43), we also see mounting evidence that we are in a state of crisis. According to scientists, the status quo can no longer be maintained and instead "rapid and far-reaching changes are needed in all aspects of society" (IPCC 2018). Lenton et al. (2019: 595) explain that "[n]o amount of economic cost–benefit analysis is going to help us. We need to change our approach to the climate problem." Ripple et al. (2019: 3, 4) and the Alliance of World Scientist state that to "secure a sustainable future, we must change how we live" and "[t]he good news is that such transformative change, with social and economic justice for all, promises far greater human well-being than does business as usual." If we are indeed in a state of crisis, where the old system must be replaced, what kind of new system do we need? What changes are necessary to minimize ecological and social impacts?

What kind of change is needed?

There is a vast amount of scientific evidence supporting the reality and seriousness of both the climate and biodiversity crises. We presented only a small portion of this evidence and every week more is produced by scientists across the globe. Instead of going any further into the science supporting the realities of these crises, this book focuses on what changes are needed to address them. In other words, if we accept that we are indeed facing an unprecedented environmental crisis, how can society respond in ways that are effective and just?

There are many proposed solutions to address our environmental crisis. As we will discuss in Chapter 2, popularly discussed solutions include individual behavior changes, market-based schemes, technological innovations and efficiency gains, renewable energy creation,[1] and geoengineering. But will these be enough? Do they represent the "far-reaching" changes in all aspects of society called for by scientists? Do they represent the "transformative change" that scientists call for? In Chapter 2, we present evidence demonstrating the inadequacy of popular proposed solutions. We also illustrate exactly why these proposed solutions will not be sufficient—because they are not transformative or far-reaching and, most critically, they fail to address the root driver of these problematic environmental conditions.

Many scientists now agree that a system prioritizing economic growth is a root driver of both the climate and biodiversity crises. Green et al. (2018: 1), representing nearly 100 scientists, argue that governments have betrayed us "in failing to acknowledge that infinite economic growth on a planet with finite resources is non-viable." Steffen et al. (2018: 5–6) state that "[t]he present dominant socioeconomic system, however, is based on high-carbon economic growth and exploitative resource use" and we need "changes in behavior, technology and innovation, governance, and values." The IPBES summary report (2019a: 10) similarly explains:

> A key component of sustainable pathways is the evolution of global financial and economic systems to build a global sustainable economy, steering away from the current, limited paradigm of economic growth... It would also entail a shift beyond standard economic indicators such as gross domestic product to include those able to capture more holistic, long-term views of economics and quality of life.

Lastly, Ripple et al. (2019: 4) state that:

> Excessive extraction of materials and overexploitation of ecosystems, driven by economic growth, must be quickly curtailed to maintain long-term sustainability of the biosphere ... Our goals need to shift from GDP growth and the pursuit of affluence toward sustaining ecosystems and improving human well-being by prioritizing basic needs and reducing inequality.

Why are these scientists focusing so much on GDP? GDP stands for Gross Domestic Product and represents the market value of all goods and services produced in a specific time period. GDP was created as an indicator during World War II, aimed to assess productive capabilities for the war effort. Increasing GDP annually was then widely adopted as a global economic goal, with average yearly increases in the US of around 3%. That means every year more and more goods are produced and services offered.

However, producing an ever-increasing amount of goods and services each year continues to require an increasing amount of materials and energy. It therefore makes sense that a GDP growth of 1% equals a 0.6% growth in material use (Wiedmann et al. 2015) and a 1% increase in GDP equals a 0.5–0.7% increase in carbon emissions (Burke et al. 2015). It also makes sense that the most notable carbon emissions reductions have occurred during economic recession due to a reduction in production and consumption (Feng et al. 2015). Based on their analyses of carbon budgets, Anderson and Bows (2011) find that overall reductions in economic growth are necessary to effectively address climate change.

In terms of biodiversity loss, the production of goods drives higher rates of extraction and use of resources impacting land use, habitat, hunting/harvesting, pollution, invasive species, and climate change—all major drivers of extinction (Ceballos et al. 2017; IPBES 2019a; Otero et al. 2020). The production of beef, soybeans, and biofuels (Rudell et al. 2009) drives deforestation in the tropics, the leading cause of terrestrial extinction (Sodhi et al. 2009). In addition, globalized trade has resulted in the proliferation of invasive species (Mooney and Hobbs 2000; Otero et al. 2020). Czech et al. (2012) and Sol's (2019) analyses reveal a strong positive association between GDP growth and species endangerment. In a 2020 review, Otero et al. illustrate how economic growth increases resource use, trade, land use change, climate change, and invasive species—all contributing to biodiversity loss. As the United Nations biodiversity chief Paşca Palmer explains, this means that to address the biodiversity crisis, "[w]e need a transformation in the way we consume and produce" (Conley 2019). Scientists increasingly agree that to address climate change and biodiversity loss we need to rethink and even recreate our economic system.

Questioning economic growth

The science illustrates that it is not GDP growth that results in increased carbon emissions and species extinction, but the increase in material and energy use associated with economic growth. Thus, many people have turned to the idea of *decoupling* to address this problematic relationship. Decoupling, in absolute terms, would mean creating a production system where economic growth could increase without increasing environmental impacts. Yet, as we will detail in Chapter 3, absolute decoupling remains elusive in terms of resource use and much too slow in terms of reducing carbon emissions (Hickel and Kallis 2019; Schor and Jorgenson 2019). Those who continue to defend decoupling and the idea of "green growth" largely rely upon data that fails to take into account imported goods and system complexities beyond national borders (see Knight and Schor 2014; Schor and Jorgenson 2019).

What the evidence shows is that absolute decoupling for materials is likely impossible and that absolute decoupling of carbon emissions is nowhere near the rates necessary (Hickel and Kallis 2019). What decoupling does provide is a useful concept to rationalize the continuation of GDP growth and wealth accumulation for a relatively small portion of the population: in 2017, the wealthiest 1% of individuals held 82% of all global wealth (Oxfam 2018). A small subset of the population has greatly benefited from a system that prioritizes economic growth, but this system is now increasingly putting all people in danger. Given that decoupling as a solution remains elusive in reality, reliance on the idea is a risky approach as our environmental crisis continues to escalate (Schor and Jorgenson 2019).

A key idea in this debate is biophysical limits. Scientists and economists have long disputed the existence of biophysical or planetary limits. If we assume there are no limits, then we can continue to prioritize never-ending economic growth and the extraction, production, and consumption to support that growth. If we believe that there are limits, however, then we need to modify our social systems in ways that stay within these limits or we end up in "ecological overshoot" or exceeding safe "planetary boundaries" (Rockstrom 2009).

Ecological economists, scientists, and environmentalists increasingly argue that our current use of natural resources and energy already surpasses the Earth's biophysical limits (e.g., Jackson 2009; Daly 2013). According to Rockstrom (2009), we have already surpassed boundaries related to the nitrogen cycle, biodiversity, and climate (Steffen et al. 2015). Based on the ecological footprint concept, Earth Overshoot Day represents the day each year that humanity uses more resources and services than can be regenerated in a year. Every year that day comes earlier. As explained by Pope Francis (EOD 2019):

> The fact that has shocked me the most is the Overshoot Day: by July 29th, we used up all the regenerative resources of 2019. From July 30 we started to consume more resources than the planet can regenerate in a year. It's very serious. It's a global emergency.

Schmelzer (2015) argues that the cause of overshoot is economic growth and "increasing levels of material production run up to the ecological limits of a finite planet." Scientists also agree that never-ending economic growth on a finite planet is "non-viable" (Green et al. 2018). While we are not yet seeing global resource shortages in line with neo-Malthusian projections, the climate and biodiversity crises represent warning signs of the non-viability of our current trajectory.

If we accept that we must live within biophysical limits, we then need to reduce production and consumption levels in places where people are over-producing and over-consuming, namely wealthy countries. In these wealthy countries, the goal of increasing GDP has resulted in increased marketing and the production of unnecessary and purposefully short-lived goods (Hickel 2019a). As material production has continued to increase in these countries, advertising encourages people to buy more additional goods and credit cards and debt enable these purchases. Yet data continues to show that after basic human needs are met, additional material goods do not increase happiness and/or well-being (Easterlin et al. 2010). Despite technological innovations and productivity gains, work time has increased to produce more and more goods per person (Circle Economy 2020). Rauch (2000) estimated that if we lived off of the productivity from a 40-hour work week in 1975 we would only need to work 23 hours per week, and if we lived off of 1950 productivity levels we would only need to work 11 hours per week. We are working more to produce more and have more, but we are not any happier and we are heading deeper into crises.

Does prioritizing economic growth make sense? Kallis (2015a) argues that the idea of never-ending economic growth is "absurd" and explains, "if the Egyptians had started with one cubic metre of stuff and grew it by 4.5% per year, by the end of their 3,000-year civilization, they would have occupied 2.5 billion solar systems." In terms of entropy law, researchers have quantitatively illustrated the "thermodynamic impossibility" of never-ending economic growth and deemed it irresponsible to continue on the current trajectory (Earp and Romeiro 2015: 643). Even with a reasonable assumption of technological innovation and the substitution of resources, their analysis indicates a catastrophic outcome if we maintain the status quo.

The possibly catastrophic outcomes bring into question the moral implications of economic growth. Given the uncertainties of future technological and economic developments, is it moral to assume we will find ways to continue to support economic growth? If we follow the precautionary principle, the appropriate approach would be to assume that there are biophysical limits and unknown thresholds and to act accordingly to reduce the risk of surpassing them. If we act, we could also change our system in ways that could be socially beneficial. Even if the risks of these crises are overstated, we could still benefit from changing our system in the ways necessary to address them. Therefore, the risks associated with assuming there are versus there are no biophysical limits are substantially different and have vast moral implications.

If, despite the increasing evidence, world leaders continue to act as if there are no biophysical limits and prioritize economic growth before addressing our environmental crisis, the projected impacts would be unequally experienced and result in clear injustice in terms of racial, economic, intergenerational, and inter-species justice. The rise of a youth climate change movement has brought new attention to the intergenerational injustice of these crises and activists are calling out the immorality of the economic growth paradigm. For example, 16-year-old Swedish climate activist, Greta Thunberg spoke to the United Nations, stating:

People are suffering. People are dying. Entire ecosystems are collapsing. We are in the beginning of a mass extinction. And all they can talk about is money and fairytales of eternal economic growth. How dare you!

If we listen to the scientists and acknowledge the improbability of "science fiction" level technology saving us from the environmental crisis (Earp and Romeiro 2015: 649), then continuing with the status quo becomes clearly immoral. Mounting evidence more than justifies deeply questioning economic growth and examining alternative paths forward.

Degrowth for a better future?

We, the authors, are three social scientists who have been studying environmental issues for many years, especially issues related to climate change, biodiversity conservation, and agriculture. After studying social and ecological impacts and identifying the causes and drivers of these impacts, we were left questioning the adequacy of dominantly proposed solutions and seeking more effective alternatives. Upon being convinced by the evidence that the economic growth imperative is a key driver of the problems we study, we stumbled upon a whole body of literature and scholarship presenting another way forward: degrowth.

We approach degrowth from a position of great concern over how to justly address our climate and biodiversity crises. We are convinced that a system prioritizing economic growth is a key driver of these crises, so we seek to understand how we can change our society to move away from growth. Degrowth is a planned downscaling of production and consumption in wealthy, overconsuming countries to transition to a steady-state economy that exists within biophysical limits and can be sustained. It is living with enough and reproducing that level of enough, not producing more and more for the sake of GDP growth. It is working less, producing less, and consuming less unnecessary things. Degrowth also has the potential to substantially increase equality, health, and well-being. There are also legitimate questions and concerns about degrowth, including the use of the term "degrowth," which we will discuss later in this book.

Degrowth does not aim to decrease GDP but abandons it as a societal goal and aims to reduce the material and energy throughput pushing us over biophysical limits. In this way, it would alleviate many of the stressors causing the climate and biodiversity crises. It would also present an opportunity to restructure society around new goals aimed at improving social and ecological well-being. Jackson (2009) argues that due to ecological limits it is not a matter of *if* the economy will contract but *when*. With degrowth, we can choose a transition to a more sustainable system rather than wait for the climate and biodiversity crises to trigger possible economic and social collapse.

In the following chapters, we examine how a degrowth transition could address our climate and biodiversity crises. We transparently take a normative position: protecting current and future generations of humans and other species is important and a worthy reason to rethink our social and economic system. In Chapter 2, we summarize evidence showing that mainstream solutions to these crises are insufficient. In Chapter 3, we present evidence that challenges the economic growth paradigm and illustrates the problems in continuing with the status quo. Chapter 4 describes degrowth, including key principles, policy proposals, and associated lifestyle changes. Chapter 5 discusses some of the primary critiques of degrowth. Our final chapter examines how a degrowth transition might actually come about and the challenges and opportunities moving forward.

Our overall goal in this book is to examine degrowth as a way to minimize the impacts associated with our environmental crisis and to offer a more just future. While we will present substantial evidence that supports a degrowth transition, we will also at times take critical positions and question certain proposals and ideas. Our overall examination focuses on what might result in the best possible future. We are indeed in a clear state of crisis: it is a decisive moment and a crucial time in history, we face serious dangers and challenges ahead, our decisions today will have far-reaching impacts into the future, and our current system can no longer be maintained. In this book, we examine degrowth as an alternative to address this crisis and support a better future. Gills and Morgan (2019: 13), argue "We need to start thinking about degrowth as responsible and not radical. We need to start thinking of it as the realistic option." This book aims to further the consideration of degrowth as a viable alternative and to examine how it could be used to create a more sustainable and just future.

Note

1 We refer to the inadequacy of renewable energy creation without reducing fossil fuel use and total energy consumption—see Chapter 2.

2   Beyond false solutions

A primary reason to consider degrowth as a response to the climate and biodiversity crises is the mounting evidence illustrating that other proposed solutions will either be insufficient or too risky and therefore represent "false solutions." While some current solutions do indeed offer positive contributions, they remain insufficient because the economic growth imperative undermines their potential. Solutions that ignore the relationship between the system that drives economic growth and our environmental crisis leave the primary driver intact.

The false solutions we examine here include individual behavioral changes (without changing the social systems in which individual behaviors are structured), market-based solutions through carbon pricing, improving energy and carbon efficiency (without pursuing total reductions in energy consumption), expanding renewable energy (but not simultaneously reducing fossil fuel use and total energy consumption), and lastly geoengineering (which is too risky). The first two mainstream solutions are common in both climate change and biodiversity efforts while the last three are specific to climate change. Some of these solutions overlap. For example, many suggested individual behavioral changes are "market-based solutions" in that they recommend changes in consumptive habits, assuming that this will influence market dynamics in environmentally beneficial ways.

We have purposefully chosen the straightforward and polemical term "false solutions" because alone these solutions are empty promises. They are "false" either because they are (1) inadequate or (2) too risky and (3) divert attention and funding away from adequate, more just, and less risky solutions. By "inadequate," we mean the solution is characterized by one or more of the following:

Too slow or small in impact to meet prominent emissions reductions targets.

Too slow or small in impact to dramatically slow or halt biodiversity loss.

Paradoxically increases environmental pressure (as in the case of the "Jevons paradox").

One of the false solutions, solar geoengineering, may have the potential to adequately address global warming but is simply too risky to pursue when compared to alternative pathways.

Our other criterion of a false solution, that it diverts attention and funding from adequate solutions, deserves qualification. Some of these solutions, especially individual behavioral changes and the expansion of renewable energy, are essential for a degrowth transition if combined with the strategies outlined in Chapter 5. For example, changing the individual behaviors of large groups of people is of critical importance to significantly reduce carbon emissions and slow or halt biodiversity loss. We do not object to changing individual behaviors, but given the evidence we do not believe that changing individual behaviors within the current social formation will meet ecological goals and are also skeptical of the assumption that changes in individual behaviors will lead to system-level changes. The following sections summarize the inadequacies and/or risks of these solutions and provide evidence that they divert funding and attention away from more effective and less risky solutions.

Individual behavioral changes

The call to "go green" usually implies changing our lifestyle and everyday routines to address environmental problems, including switching to energy-efficient lightbulbs, weatherproofing homes, driving less or buying a hybrid car, carpooling, taking shorter showers, and buying "greener" products. Yet increasing evidence shows that individual behavioral changes are inadequate responses to our environmental crisis and, more importantly, divert attention, and even reduce support for, more effective system-altering responses.

We recognize there are clear benefits to adopting environmentally friendly behaviors. However, as a solution (1) greening one's lifestyle is inadequate when pursued alone or even when paired with other false solutions, (2) the focus on individual consumptive practices misunderstands relations between production and consumption and reproduces the social system that drives biodiversity loss and climate change, and, most importantly, (3) the narrow focus on changing lifestyles in mainstream narratives overlooks the structural basis of the ecological crisis, thereby diverting attention from more effective and just solutions.

While we are unaware of any empirical studies that assess the effectiveness or ineffectiveness of lifestyle changes on biodiversity conservation, there is evidence of their inadequacy for addressing climate change, also a known driver of biodiversity loss. Individual-to household-level changes have been estimated to be able to reduce emissions by around 7% (Dietz et al. 2009) to 22% (Jensen 2009) in the US. However, to avoid catastrophic warming and limit warming to 1.5°C, the US should reach net-zero emissions by 2030 (Climate Action Tracker 2019). Lifestyle changes within the existing system cannot reduce emissions at the rate and scale necessary to avoid catastrophic warming. It is important to again emphasize that we are not against individual behavioral changes, we are merely pointing out that they are insufficient, as supporters of this strategy know (Dietz et al. 2009).

A second reason individual behavioral changes are a false solution is due to the focus on changing consumptive behavior. "Going green" often means "shopping green." However, as Galbraith (1958) and others (Schnaiberg 1980) argued long ago, production drives consumption, primarily through advertising and the creation of false needs via the culture industry (Marcuse 1964; Horkheimer and Adorno 1969). A system that requires constant growth must keep expanding production and also increase consumption to create buyers for more and more products. The focus on "greening" consumption cannot address this relationship because it assumes the relationship is inverted (i.e., that consumption drives production). Relatedly, the marketed "greenness" of most green commodities is questionable. For example, food, textile, and woods-products companies who use at least one form of "sustainable sourcing practice" (52%) (e.g., third-party organic certification) typically only address one or a few inputs (71%) and rarely address environmental issues (Thorlakson et al. 2018).

The third and most important reason individual behavioral change should be considered a false solution is that this focus diverts attention away from the structural and system-level changes needed to adequately address our environmental crisis (Brulle and Dunlap 2015). As Szasz argues in *Shopping our way to safety* (2007), the attempt to protect ourselves from environmental hazards through shopping leads to "political anesthesia," or "a false sense of security undercutting political support for reform," thereby reproducing the existing social order (Szasz 2007: 202). For example, the option of implementing household actions to reduce emissions makes people less likely to support carbon taxes (Werfel 2017). Further, there is empirical evidence that individual behavioral changes may have other counterintuitive effects: when recycling options are available people increase resource use (Catlin and

Wang 2013) and purchasing "green" products leads to less altruistic actions (Mazar and Zhong 2010). Relatedly, the financial savings gained from reducing one's carbon footprint often fund other activities that act to shift the impacts elsewhere (Wapner and Willoughby 2005).

Market-based solutions

Market-based solutions are common in both climate change and biodiversity policy. In climate change policy, carbon markets usually consist of cap-and-trade and or carbon offset programs, implemented or under consideration in many regions from city to interstate levels, including Australia, California, the European Union (EU), New Zealand, Quebec, Canada, and South Korea (Muûls et al. 2016). Cap-and-trade programs set emissions limits and freely distribute or auction off "allowances" to emit to companies, who then trade their right to pollute, while carbon offset programs allow emitters to invest in carbon mitigation projects, many in developing countries, to "offset" their own carbon emissions.

The largest and longest continuous carbon market is the EU Emissions Trading System (ETS). Assessments of the EU ETS vary considerably depending on methodological choices (see Martin et al. 2016), ranging from the argument that most reductions in emissions resulted from other factors such as the global financial crisis and expanded renewable energy (Nicolas et al. 2014) to a 2.4–4.7% reduction in total emissions from 2005 to 2007 along with slight decreases in emission intensity during Phase II (2008–2012) (see Muûls et al. 2016: 5). A more favorable recent study estimates a ~10% decrease in emissions between 2005 and 2012 in four participating countries (France, the Netherlands, Norway, and the UK) at a firm-level, specifically when comparing the emissions of non-ETS installations to ETS installations (e.g., power stations). In other words, even the most favorable assessment does not analyze all countries, merely compares dirtier installations to slightly less (a tenth less) dirty installations and does not analyze the ETS's impact on total emissions (Dechezleprêtre et al. 2018). Along with insufficient reductions in emissions, carbon markets have led to paradoxical and even scandalous outcomes, including accidentally incentivizing firms involved in a carbon offset scheme to produce more of a highly potent greenhouse gas byproduct (HFC-23) in order to destroy it to gain emissions credits to sell to polluters (for review, see Klein 2014).

Coupled with their negligible impacts, a more important reason that carbon markets should be understood as false solutions is they reproduce the system that drives climate change and divert attention from alternative social solutions (e.g., Lohmann 2005, 2010; Foster et al. 2009; Stuart et al. 2019). This is not only a theoretical argument. Lohmann (2005) shows how the Kyoto Protocol's emphasis on emissions trading, pushed by the US who ironically did not ratify the treaty, redirected attention in the form of intellectual and financial resources from alternative policies and social changes that have the potential to actually significantly reduce emissions. Criticisms of the Protocol in favor of strong policies were scorned as a "do-nothing" stance. Similarly, a corporate watchdog non-profit makes the case that the mere existence of the EU ETS continues to undermine the ability of new emissions regulations to take hold (Corporate Europe Observatory 2015).

Market-based solutions are also common in biodiversity conservation, from biodiversity offsets—where the degradation of habitats, species, ecosystem functions, etc. in one location are "offset" in another location (Bull et al. 2013)—to ecotourism, where ecologically minded tourists supposedly create incentives for residents to engage in nature conservation (Duffy 2008). Not only is the actual effectiveness of "neoliberal conservation" dubious, the underlying problem with these approaches is they reproduce and expand the system that drives biodiversity loss (Igoe and Brockington 2007; Brockington and Duffy 2010; Igoe et al. 2010; Büscher et al. 2012). The destruction of nature due to profit accumulation is interpreted as a new accumulation strategy, which has contradictory outcomes.

Robertson's (2004, 2006) analysis of wetland mitigation banking serves as an excellent illustration. A "No Net Loss to Wetlands" policy was put in place under the George H.W. Bush administration, with the aim of total wetland acreage remaining constant by "offsetting" degraded wetlands in different geographical areas. The policy allowed developers to buy "wetland mitigation credits" from owners of an undeveloped wetland or companies who restore degraded wetlands ("wetland mitigation banks"). A developer who fills a wetland to build condos, for example, can buy wetland credits from an off-site mitigation bank. Quantifying and commensurating the "value" lost at the development site and the "value" gained at the mitigation banking site created a contradiction. Mitigation banks measured their value-gained as "bundles" of "ecological functions" while acreage was the proxy measure for bundles of ecological functions at the development site. The mitigation banks began to opportunistically exploit created ecological functions (i.e., superfluous fabricated markets) which clashed with the mitigation permit market's need for quantitative abstraction (Robertson 2004).

While individual behavior changes and market-based solutions are common in climate and biodiversity conservation, the next three false solutions—efficiency gains, renewable energy without rapid reductions in fossil fuel use, and geoengineering—are all specific to climate policy—yet as stated earlier, climate change also drives biodiversity loss.

Energy and carbon efficiency

Because of its ubiquity in climate policy, it may strike the reader as strange to label improving energy efficiency (energy use per dollar) and carbon efficiency (emissions per dollar) as "false solutions." The goals of improving efficiency or, put differently, reducing carbon intensity, are so widespread in climate change discourse that they are taken for granted. However, there is a fundamental limitation of this approach: the Jevons paradox.

The Jevons paradox—named after the economist William Stanley Jevons for his finding that improved efficiency of steam engines increased total coal consumption (Clark and Foster 2001)—refers to a commonly found association between increased resource use despite improved efficiency (e.g., Alcott 2005; Sorrell 2007; Polimini et al. 2008; York et al. 2009, 2011; York 2010; Clement 2011; York and McGee 2016). The Jevons paradox is a paradox because the usual assumption is that improvements in efficiency will decrease total resource use because fewer resources are used per economic unit. To be clear, not all "rebound effects"—when the benefits of efficiency gains are partially or fully consumed by changes in resource use—are "backfires," rebound effects above 100% (Santarius 2012). Further, the Jevons paradox refers to an association between improved efficiency and increased emissions, which is not necessarily a causal association (York and McGee 2016). However, causal drivers have been identified, including improvements in efficiency reducing prices per economic unit, which increases the use of the given resource or investment in the use of other resources (for review, see Santarius 2012; York and McGee 2016).

Regardless of the magnitude of the rebound effect and the causal drivers of the Jevons paradox, it is clear that improving efficiency is an inadequate route to tackle climate change for the simple reason that, in general, global carbon efficiency has improved while total emissions increased (York 2010). Nations with higher levels of efficiency generally have higher rates of CO_2 emissions, electricity consumption, and energy use (York and McGee 2016). In the US, individual state emissions increase in general despite improving carbon intensity by around 30% (Clement 2011).

The data are clear that improving energy and carbon efficiency is associated with counterintuitive results. Then why is a reliance on efficiency still so common in climate policy? One reason is that it appeals to economic interests. Following the US's non-ratification of the Kyoto Protocol despite getting what they wanted (carbon markets) (see above), the George W. Bush administration then turned to carbon intensity as a more economically friendly climate change strategy, one that allows for and even encourages continued economic growth and does not restrict future emissions (i.e., does not impose any real cap) (Roberts and Parks 2006: 142ff). This approach appeals to economic interests and reproduces and expands rather than challenges the drivers of climate change precisely because economic growth and emissions are linked (see Chapter 3). For the latter reason, coupled with the problem of the Jevons paradox, improving efficiency in the current system remains a false solution.

Renewable energy without reducing fossil fuel use and total energy consumption

To be clear at the outset of this section, we support the development of renewable energy (see Gunderson et al. 2018c). A massive expansion of renewable energy, especially in wind and solar, is a prerequisite to a sustainable society that supports relatively large-scale human organizations. While renewables have their own negative environmental impacts that are often ignored (Zehner 2012), these impacts are negligible compared to the continued use of fossil fuels. Renewable energy is a false solution only when it is promoted without also (1) promoting reductions in fossil fuels and (2) reductions in total energy consumption. We discuss each point below.

Calls for the expansion of renewables often assume that one new unit of renewable energy will displace one unit of fossil fuel-based energy. However, this is not the case. Only a "very modest" displacement of fossil fuel-generated energy sources with renewable energy sources occurred in the last five decades in most countries (York 2012). The problem is made clear by York and Bell (2019): fossil fuel development has steadily increased despite the comparably slight expansion of renewables. In fact, without simultaneously reducing fossil fuel development, renewable energy development may contribute to increases in energy use by increasing supply, thereby spurring demand (Zehner 2012; York 2016). As long as the call to expand renewables does not explicitly tackle the problem of the simultaneous expansion of fossil fuels and renewables, renewables will remain a false solution.

A second common oversight in the climate policy emphasis on expanding renewable energy is the fact that renewables have much lower energy return on energy invested (EROEI) ratios (e.g., 60:1 for coal compared to 18:1 for wind and 6:1 for solar) (Hall et al. 2014). This means that the amount of usable energy output (energy return) relative to the energy that went into procuring that energy (energy invested) is much lower for renewables than fossil fuels. Further, renewables have lower power densities, meaning that they take up more space than fossil fuel sources (e.g., wind and solar require around 90–100 times more area than natural gas) (van Zalk and Behrens 2018; for summary, see Leiden University 2018).

Neither lower EROEI ratios nor lower power densities are reasons to avoid transitioning to renewables. However, for these reasons and others, it is unlikely that a nearly 100% renewable energy supply is possible in a constantly growing economy and, instead, would require reductions in total energy use and a smaller overall economy (Trainer 2007; Kallis 2017; Hickel 2019a; see Chapter 5). To clarify, rapidly developing renewables is critical, yet to be an effective solution it must also be accompanied by simultaneous and significant reductions in fossil fuel development and overall reductions in energy consumption.

Geoengineering

"Geoengineering" or "climate engineering" refers to "a broad set of methods and technologies that aim to deliberately alter the climate system in order to alleviate impacts of climate change" (Boucher et al. 2013). There are two broad categories of geoengineering strategies: (1) Carbon Dioxide Removal (CDR) or "carbon geoengineering," strategies to remove CO_2 from the atmosphere or at sources of fossil fuel combustion[1] and sequestering it underground or under the ocean (U.S. National Research Council 2015a) and (2) Solar Radiation Management (SRM) or "solar geoengineering," strategies to redirect incoming solar radiation back into space (U.S. National Research Council 2015b). These strategies are appealing to many as they are framed as "quick-fix," easy, and cheap solutions to the climate crisis (Gunderson et al. 2018b, 2019).

While we do not review all carbon and solar geoengineering strategies here (e.g., The Royal Society 2009; U.S. National Research Council 2015a, 2015b; Zhang et al. 2015), we focus on the two most widely discussed techniques from each category: bioenergy with carbon capture and storage (BECCS), a form of carbon geoengineering, and stratospheric aerosol injection (SAI), a form of solar geoengineering. We make the case that BECCS is currently too ineffective to be considered a viable climate change strategy, at least in the short term, and SAI is far too risky to be considered a viable response. We then argue that geoengineering diverts attention and resources away from more effective and safer alternatives.

BECCS is a carbon geoengineering strategy based on burning crops for power generation ("bioenergy"), such as big trees, and, while burning them in power stations, capturing and storing the carbon emissions ("with carbon capture and storage") (Fridahl 2017). The approach is appealing because plants are carbon sinks, which reduces atmospheric CO_2 and CCS would prevent the carbon released when burning these plants from reentering the atmosphere. In theory, the outcome would be negative emissions (Pour et al. 2017). The bulk of empirical evidence is from separate bioenergy and CCS facilities and a single ethanol-based BECCS demonstration plant (Anderson and Peters 2016; Turner et al. 2018). In other words, the technology remains largely unproven (see Fuss et al. 2014).

Another major barrier facing BECCS is locating suitable land area to grow biomass crops—requiring acreage up to three times the size of India to meet climate goals (Anderson 2015; for other barriers, see Baik et al. 2018; Turner et al. 2018). This much area used for growing bioenergy crops may compete with land used for food crops (National Academies of Sciences, Engineering, and Medicine 2018). For these reasons and others, BECCS has been called a "dangerous distraction" (Fuss et al. 2014) and "high-stakes gamble" (Anderson and Peters 2016: 183) that diverts attention away from tested and effective mitigation strategies.

SAI, the most prominently discussed solar geoengineering strategy due to its low cost, is a proposal to inject sulfur particles into the stratosphere to redirect incoming solar radiation back into space (Keith 2013; U.S. National Research Council 2015b). It is the only strategy we categorize as a "false solution" on the grounds that it is far too risky. Risks include unknown impacts on weather, plants, and clouds; the potential for droughts and famine; potential to exacerbate the ozone hole; an increase in acid rain and air pollution; problems emanating from potential commercial control and military use; and, most frighteningly, the possibility for a "termination effect," where, if SAI cannot be maintained after being implemented, temperatures could increase rapidly due to a build-up of background emissions (see Robock 2008a, 2008b; Robock et al. 2009, 2010; Boucher et al. 2013; Ferraro et al. 2014).

In addition to its serious risks, which could permanently alter global cycles, SAI is also a false solution because it diverts attention away from more effective and just responses. While solar geoengineering scientists push for increasing mitigation efforts and are usually cautious about their support for geoengineering (Reynolds et al. 2016), there is good reason to anticipate that SAI may be implemented in order to reproduce the current social priorities and system that drives climate change (Gunderson et al. 2019). Not only are economic justifications for SAI common (e.g., that it is much cheaper than reducing emissions), which will appeal to those with the power to implement climate policy, but there is some evidence of support for SAI from the elite (e.g., Bill Gates), fossil fuel industry representatives, and even climate denialist organizations (e.g., the Heartland Institute) (Hamilton 2013; Gunderson et al. 2019). SAI could very well rationalize the continued extraction and use of fossil fuels (Gunderson et al. 2019).

While individual geoengineering strategies must be evaluated separately and we find some forms of carbon geoengineering to have some potential to reduce carbon concentrations if embedded in different social conditions (see Stuart et al. 2020), geoengineering currently is broadly labeled a false solution here due to its reliance on untested technology and, in the case of SAI, association with unjustifiable risks. Further, geoengineering strategies divert attention and resources away from effective and just climate change solutions.

Addressing systemic contradictions

This chapter argues that commonly discussed solutions to biodiversity loss and climate change are "false solutions" in the sense that they are inadequate and divert attention away from more effective and just solutions or, in the case of SAI, are far too risky and divert attention away from more just and less risky solutions. We conclude with a brief explanation as to why these approaches are likely to continue to be inadequate.

Mainstream climate policy leaves the current social priorities and system unquestioned or assumes its unchangeability and/or desirability. However, as we explain in Chapter 3, it is the basic structures and dynamics of our current social and economic system—prioritizing economic growth—that drives climate change and biodiversity loss. These solutions will remain inadequate because their implementation does not transform but, instead, reproduces the social order that accelerates our environmental crisis. The problem with reproducing rather than transforming the contemporary model of society is that it also reproduces fundamental social-ecological contradictions that are intrinsic to the dynamics of this model. In Chapter 5, we further examine these contradictions and how growth relates to capitalism as well as socialism.

Failing to get at the engine that keeps driving us deeper into crisis undermines the potential of solutions. For example, efficiency and renewable energy have the potential to reduce total emissions, but in an economy that must grow the result is an overall increase in energy use and emissions. As we examine in later chapters, in a system that does not require increasing levels of production and consumption, these solutions can play a key role in addressing our environmental crisis. However, a prerequisite to their effective implementation is abandoning the economic growth imperative that continues to constrain their potential.

Note

1 It is debated whether carbon capture at sources of fossil fuel combustion (usually power plants) should be labeled a mitigation or geoengineering strategy (see Vaughan and Lenton 2011).

3 The case against economic growth

As mainstream solutions to the climate and biodiversity crises are increasingly deemed insufficient and leading scientists continue to identify economic growth as a key driver of these crises, it seems plausible that society may reconsider prioritizing economic growth. However, there remains substantial social and political resistance to the notion that growth is harmful. Economic growth as something desirable and "good" for society has been normalized to the degree that many people cannot imagine a world with different priorities. The underlying belief that a prosperous society must always have increasing wealth accumulation supports a system with ever increasing levels of production, sales, and consumption. The assumption is that this production-consumption engine must keep going or else the whole system will breakdown. Yet the data reveals that the vast majority of wealth created from this system continues to go to a small portion of the population, while the ongoing production-consumption engine is driving us all further into environmental crisis and toward possible social collapse.

As stated by Hickel and Kallis (2019: 15), "As scientists we should not let political expediency shape our view of facts. We should assess the facts and then draw conclusions, rather than start with palatable conclusions and ignore inconvenient facts." For those faithful to the idea of never-ending economic growth, we present three key reasons to question these convictions. First, evidence from the past and present suggests that life with less or no economic growth can be prosperous in terms of social and ecological well-being and that prioritizing GDP growth can actually reduce measures of standards of living and social well-being. Therefore, we should deeply question the assumption that GDP growth is a requirement for a thriving society.

Second, there is substantial evidence illustrating that GDP is positively correlated with material and energy use, carbon emissions, environmental degradation, and species extinction. The dominant solution to address this problematic relationship is "decoupling" economic growth from environmental harm (via green growth), yet research shows that there is no evidence of the necessary decoupling in material resource use and no evidence supporting that the decoupling of carbon emissions can be accomplished at the rate necessary to meet the IPCC's 1.5°C or 2°C targets (Hickel and Kallis 2019; Parrique et al. 2019; Schor and Jorgenson 2019).

Beyond the empirical evidence, a third argument focuses on the moral implications of increasing GDP growth when the known risks of doing so are great and there are no existing solutions to sufficiently address these risks. The likely impacts to current and future generations of humans and other species are severe and irreversible. We discuss the moral implications of relying on the unproven idea of rapid decoupling and promoting the ideology of green growth. Should we err on the side caution, even when it goes against indoctrinated ideas of progress?

These three arguments are described and supported below. We especially draw from several key recent publications (Hickel and Kallis 2019; Parrique et al. 2019; Schor and Jorgenson 2019) that more clearly and convincingly support these arguments than any previous evidence. Lastly, we illustrate how these arguments lead us towards the conclusion that an overall reduction in production and consumption in line with "degrowth," is a necessary pathway to best protect current and future generations of humans and other species from an otherwise catastrophic trajectory.

Do we need economic growth?

The economy is generally defined as the production, distribution, and consumption of resources—or the use of material resources to satisfy human needs or values (Kallis 2018). Economies have existed for thousands of years using systems of reciprocity, sharing, barter, or money as the basis of resource exchange. We can imagine a society with an economy that does not include the concept of accumulating profit, where resources are exchanged, given, traded, or shared based on need. If poverty is a lack of profit accumulation, then this society would be deemed poor. But if poverty is a lack of food, shelter, leisure time, health, and well-being, then this could be a very wealthy society.

For thousands of years economies existed without continual accumulation of wealth and material goods, yet for the past 200 years the global economy has been increasingly geared toward growing levels of accumulation. Our modern economy is defined by this prioritization of never-ending profit and wealth accumulation rather than the exchange of resources for use (see Chapter 5). This is the ultimate driver of growth, as more goods and services sold increases profit accumulation. Increasing the production of goods and services may seem justified to meet the needs of a growing population, yet as we detail below, resource use per person has increased. Increased consumption is necessary for the increased production and sales to support greater levels of profit accumulation. However, this does not mean that wealth is accumulated equally or that everyone has the resources they need (see Hickel 2017).

To support rising levels of profit accumulation, there has been an increase in human productivity as well as the total goods per person produced and consumed over time. In the past century, global per capita resource use has doubled (Parrique et al. 2019). In addition, global material use has quadrupled since 1970, growing twice as fast as the human population (Circle Economy 2020). More materials and energy are being used per person over time, far beyond what is justified based on population growth and human needs. As productivity rates have increased, prioritizing growth has mandated that these gains be invested in further production and profitability. Yet as Schor and Jorgenson (2019: 325) explain, this need not be the case:

> The optimal rate of growth depends on workers' preferences for goods and leisure. If workers want to take their productivity growth in the form of shorter hours, the labor market will equilibrate with fewer hours supplied.

We should not assume a system with increasing levels of accumulation is a "natural" system simply because we are accustomed to it. Although the primary driver of increases in material and energy throughput is the structural characteristics of our current economic system (see Chapter 5), it is critical that we understand the origins of GDP growth as a social priority and also question if it should remain a priority.

It was not until the 1950s that economic growth in terms of GDP became a policy priority for the US and other nations (Victor 2010). The concept of GDP emerged during the Great Depression when Simon Kuznets was asked to create a way to track the productive power of a country. GDP was specifically used during World War II to assess productivity for the war effort. Yet, after the war ended, policymakers continued to use GDP as a positive indicator based on the assumption that if people are making and buying goods at an increasing rate, then society is flourishing. However, as quoted in Semuels (2016) even Kuznets doubted the use of GDP in this way, warning: "[t]he welfare of a nation can scarcely be inferred from a measure of national income." Despite Kuznets' skepticism, GDP has remained the primary indicator of social progress and the goal of increasing GDP has driven global policy.

Do high levels of GDP growth indicate that a society is flourishing? Increasing evidence suggests it does not. Despite an average 3% increase in GPD in the US, at least 43 million Americans are still living in poverty, wages have not considerably increased since the 1980s and even with positive GDP growth the median income of households has declined (Semuels 2016). In addition, many countries with lower rates of GDP growth, such as Scandinavian countries, actually have higher levels of equality, health, education, and well-being. In places where ample resources are available, it makes little sense to focus on increasing production (and GDP) when remaining problems are related to distribution and the adequate provisioning of social services (Hickel 2019a).

A growing number of economists agree that GDP is a problematic indicator of progress and well-being (e.g., Victor 2010; Daly 2013; Dietz 2015; Stiglitz 2019a,b). GDP does not distinguish between costs and benefits; it only includes flows of money, not stocks of resources; it fails to include activities with no market value; and it does not provide information on how wealth is distributed. Critics point out that an event causing significant harm, such as a natural disaster or oil spill, can increase GPD. Increased production does not translate into increased social well-being. Easterlin et al. (2010), among others, have shown that economic growth that goes beyond satisfying basic needs does not lead to increased happiness. More evidence supports the position that GDP has actually undermined qualitative goals, such as social and ecological well-being (O'Neill 2012; Stiglitz 2019a). Alternative indicators, such as the Index of Sustainable Economic Welfare and the General Progress Indicator, illustrate how GDP can increase while measures of well-being decrease. Relatedly, economic growth does not increase human well-being per unit of environmental pressure after a certain level of affluence (Dietz et al. 2012), despite the fact that mainstream economics views "increasing affluence . . . as essentially equivalent to human well-being" (Dietz 2015: 125). As argued by Nobel award winning economist Joseph Stiglitz (2009), not only is GDP a poor measure of well-being but "chasing GDP growth results in lower living standards."

Stiglitz has been increasingly vocal about the risks of using GDP as the primary indicator of progress, calling for alternative indicators that better support social and ecological well-being. Stigltiz (2019b) states that "we need better tools to assess economic performance and social progress" and explains that his concerns about GDP "have now been brought to the fore with the climate crisis." Her further argues "[i]f we measure the wrong thing, we will do the wrong thing." Not only is chasing GDP growth leading us further into environmental crisis, but it also prevents the flourishing of other positive conceptions of social progress. As explained by Daly (2013: 24), while it is largely believed that "without economic growth all progress is at an end . . . [o]n the contrary, without growth . . . true progress finally will have a chance."

Economic growth and our environmental crisis

Chapter 1 included many examples of leading scientists identifying GDP growth as a primary driver of the climate and biodiversity crises. While all of the examples given will not be restated here, in both cases, scientists have found positive correlations between GDP growth and environmental degradation. This makes sense when we acknowledge that increasing production results in increasing levels of resource use, pollution, and carbon emissions. GDP growth of 1% equals a 0.6% growth in material use (Wiedmann et al. 2015) and a 1% increase in GDP equals a 0.5–0.7% increase in carbon emissions (Burke et al. 2015). It is not a coincidence that the most notable reductions in carbon emissions have occurred during economic recessions (Feng et al. 2015; Hickel and Kallis 2019; Parrique et al. 2019). In addition, studies show a strong positive association between GDP growth and species endangerment (Czech et al. 2012; Sol 2019), as many activities that create wealth result in habitat loss, pollution, deforestation, and other negative impacts to a range of species (Cavlovic et al. 2000).

Despite these environmental impacts, GDP growth is defended and maintained as a global priority largely based on the concept of "decoupling" as a remedy to these problematic relationships. Decoupling refers to the idea that we can create conditions where increases in GDP do not result in negative environmental impacts. Thus, there can be "green growth." Promoting green growth through decoupling has been the primary strategy of many global governing bodies to support "progress" and "development" while addressing our escalating environmental crisis. The Organization for Economic Co-operation and Development (OECD) officially adopted decoupling as a goal in 2001 followed by the European Commission, United Nations Environment

Programme, and the World Bank (Parrique et al. 2019). Decoupling also remains a specific target in the United Nations Sustainable Development Goals (see Hickel 2019b).

Decoupling depends on the use of green technologies that are more efficient and based on alternative energy sources as well as a transition away from material goods and towards a service and information-based economy (Hoffman 2016). Jackson (2009) makes the distinction between relative and absolute decoupling. Relative decoupling refers to reduced environmental impact per unit of economic output, whereas absolute decoupling refers to the overall reduction of environmental impacts. While relative decoupling (per unit output) can be seen in many cases, increases in total production continue to increase overall environmental degradation—making absolute decoupling more elusive (Parrique et al. 2019). However, it is absolute decoupling that is necessary to reduce overall environmental impacts (Jackson 2009).

Evidence indicates that decoupling remains largely a theory rather than an empirically proven solution to the climate and biodiversity crises. Daly (2013) explains that decoupling is limited by the interdependence of production between different economic sectors and by the fact that expanding service and information sectors will not substantially reduce the use of energy and material goods. In addition, efficiency gains are not indefinite and increasing levels of production to support GDP growth undermine efficiency gains (Ward et al. 2016). Thus far, the evidence supports these explanations. Cases where absolute decoupling has been identified are often based on territorial material use or emissions, not on overall consumption which includes materials imported and carbon emissions related to imports (Knight and Schor 2014; Hickel and Kallis 2019; Parrique et al. 2019). In addition, identified decoupling in many cases is temporary and recoupling occurs when conditions change (Hickel and Kallis 2019; Parrique et al. 2019). To effectively address our environmental crisis, decoupling would need to be absolute, permanent, global, and occur at a rate fast enough to meet the IPCC's 1.5°C target (IPCC 2018).

More studies are concluding that there is no evidence that global absolute decoupling of material resource use has occurred or can occur in the future. On average, every 10% rise in GDP has been accompanied with a 6% increase in material footprint (Wiedmann et al. 2015). Efficiency gains cannot be realized when the material footprint of OECD nations has increased by 50% between 1990 and 2008—they are "trumped by increases in volume" (Parrique et al. 2019: 23). As stated by Hoffman (2016: 36), "dematerialized growth remains an illusion." The material intensity of GDP per capita increased by 60%

between 1900 and 2009 (Bithas and Kalimeris 2018). This evidence supports Hickel and Kallis' (2019: 7) conclusion that: "green growth theory—in terms of resource use—lacks empirical support." Resource use has direct implications for carbon emissions and biodiversity loss, as use of water, forests, energy, and other resources increase with GDP (Cavlovic et al. 2000; Czech et al. 2012; Sol 2019).

In terms of carbon emissions, there is limited evidence supporting the success of current decoupling efforts and mounting evidence supporting the conclusion that global decoupling cannot occur at rates fast enough to stay within 1.5°C or 2°C of warming. Jorgenson and Clark (2012) demonstrate a strong relationship between per capita carbon emissions and GDP per capita in developed nations that is stable over time. Mardani et al. (2019) illustrate a bidirectional coupling between GDP and carbon emissions. Despite carbon markets and increases in efficiency and renewable energy sources, Granados and Spash (2019) find that carbon emissions in the US are still significantly correlated with economic growth. Hickel and Kallis (2019) identify countries where territorial decoupling has occurred and state that absolute decoupling is technologically possible; however, once import-related emissions have been included almost no countries have thus far achieved permanent absolute decoupling (Schor and Jorgenson 2019).

Studies using empirical data illustrate how modest decoupling in developed nations has been a result of increased carbon-intensive production in developing nations (Jorgenson and Clark 2012; Knight and Schor 2014; Schor and Jorgenson 2019). In other words, environmental impacts are being exported. Knight and Schor (2014) report:

> While we find some reduction in the linkage between economic growth and territorial emissions, once we account for high-income countries' offshoring of emissions, there is no evidence of decoupling.

Based on mounting evidence, Parrique et al. (2019: 24) conclude that there has "never been a global pattern of absolute decoupling of CO_2 from economic growth."

Even with the possibility of absolute decoupling of carbon emissions through significant investment in energy efficiency and renewable energy, this decoupling would need to occur at a rate fast enough to keep warming from passing dangerous critical thresholds (Parrique et al. 2019). We are currently on a trajectory for warming of 4.2°C (2.5–5.5°C) by 2100, yet leading scientists argue we need to keep warming below 1.5°C (IPCC 2018). The important question then becomes:

what level and rate of decoupling is necessary to accomplish this goal? Hickel and Kallis (2019: 8) examine this question in depth and argue:

> absolute reductions in carbon emissions are possible to achieve . . . however, the objective is not simply to reduce emissions (a matter of flows), but to keep total emissions from exceeding specific carbon budgets.

This is a matter of achieving absolute decoupling at a fast-enough rate. Hickel and Kallis (2019) explain that the only climate scenarios that keep warming below 2°C rely on BECCS for negative emissions. Yet, as we argued in Chapter 2, this technology is not yet developed and assumptions about negative emissions remain unproven. Including BECCS in scenarios, however, has allowed for a larger carbon budget and continued support for green growth.

Perhaps more clearly than ever, Hickel and Kallis (2019: 10, 11) explain how absolute decoupling of carbon emissions to stay within 1.5°C or even 2°C targets while sustaining economic growth is not only highly unlikely but likely impossible:

> Without BECCS, global emissions need to fall to net zero by 2050 for 1.5°C, or by 2075 for 2°C. This entails reductions of 6.8 per cent per year and 4 per cent per year, respectively. Theoretically, this can be accomplished with (a) a rapid shift to 100 per cent renewable energy to eliminate emissions from fossil fuel combustion (Jacobson and Delucchi 2011); plus (b) afforestation and soil regeneration to eliminate emissions from land use change; plus (c) a shift to alternative industrial processes to eliminate emissions from the production of cement, steel, and plastic.
>
>   If we assume global GDP continues to grow at 3 per cent per year (the average from 2010 to 2014), then decoupling must occur at a rate of 10.5 per cent per year for 1.5°C, or 7.3 per cent per year for 2°C. If global GDP grows at 2.1 per cent per year . . . then decoupling must occur at 9.6 per cent per year for 1.5°C, or 6.4 per cent per year for 2°C. All of these targets are beyond what existing empirical models indicate is feasible.

Parrique et al. (2019: 15) agree with this conclusion, finding that if we need a 45% reduction in carbon emissions by 2030 (IPCC 2018), then "even the decrease of emissions achieved in the most successful national cases of absolute decoupling are far from being sufficient to keep global warming from passing a critical threshold." Hickel (2019a) also argues that even under the most optimistic assumptions, continued GDP growth will push us past the carbon budgets for both 1.5°C and 2°C targets. This supports Anderson and Bows (2011) earlier work illustrating that the necessary emissions reductions are incompatible with continued economic growth. Anderson estimates that as of 2019 wealthy nations need to reduce emissions by 12% per year to stay within a 2°C target (Hickel and Kallis 2019), yet emissions reductions any greater than 3–4% per year are incompatible with economic growth (Anderson and Bows 2011).

If we cast aside the unsubstantiated assumption that BECCS can be a highly effective negative emissions technology (see Chapter 2), then we are left with only one possible way to stay within the IPCC's (2018) 1.5°C target. Only one scenario in the IPCC special report (2018) did not rely on BECCS. This scenario was published by Grubler et al. (2018) and stays within 1.5°C of warming through reducing total global energy use by 40% (by 2050), reducing total global material production and consumption by 20%, afforestation projects, and dematerialization through an increase in sharing material goods and commodities (see Hickel and Kallis 2019). Given a lack of any evidence that BECCS can result in the projected negative emissions, the Grubler scenario represents a more feasible and realistic approach.

Parrique et al. (2019) make an important point: these findings in no way mean that we should oppose the efficiency gains and a transition to renewable energy that would support a decoupling strategy. In fact, these are important and even essential to reduce total carbon emissions. Yet, they are not sufficient to reduce emissions at the rate necessary. This would also require reducing total production and consumption. They promote "complementing efficiency-oriented policies with sufficiency policies, with a shift in priority and emphasis from the former to the latter even though both have a role to play" (Parrique et al. 2019: 3). In other words, as we explained in the previous chapter, the potential of our best technological solutions can only be realized if we simultaneously reduce production and consumption.

The moral implications of green growth

Green growth proponents argue that even though we currently lack concrete evidence that decoupling at the rate necessary is possible, future technological innovation will be able to rapidly increase the rate of decoupling. This faith in human technological advancement is widespread, as seen through techno-optimist and eco-modernist positions (Grunwald 2018). While we agree that there will surely be some advances in technology in the short and long term that could help to address our environmental crisis, the extent of technological advancement necessary is significant and cannot be assumed. As Parrique et al. (2019: 51) explain,

> relying only on technology to mitigate climate change implies extreme rates of eco-innovation improvements, which current trends are very far from matching, and which, to our knowledge, have never been witnessed in the history of our species.

In other words, the pace of technological evolution necessary has no precedent in human history and therefore cannot be depended upon to address the urgency of the climate crisis.

Parrique et al. (2019: 55) also identify multiple factors that are likely to impede decoupling in the future and undermine green growth as a solution. These factors include: "(1) Rising energy expenditures, (2) rebound effects, (3) problem shifting, (4) the underestimated impact of services, (5) the limited potential of recycling in a growing economy, (6) insufficient and inappropriate technological change, and (7) cost shifting." They explain each of these factors and how they undermine decoupling. Given that each of these factors independently could impede possible decoupling, together they should raise significant skepticism about green growth strategies. Parrique et al. (2019: 55) state that due to these factors, "the decoupling hypothesis appears highly compromised, if not clearly unrealistic."

Given the lack of evidence in support of sufficient decoupling as well as the many obstacles preventing a rapid green growth pathway, Hickel and Kallis (2019) and Parrique et al. (2019) support a precautionary approach. As the stakes are extremely high (e.g., possible ecological and social collapse), and the future remains incredibly uncertain (e.g., are there critical thresholds? what are they? what are the impacts?), the most responsible and moral pathway is to be cautious. Hickel and Kallis (2019: 15) explain:

> [o]ne may insist that green growth hasn't occurred because it has not been tried, the fact that it hasn't been empirically observed till now then becoming irrelevant. We follow instead a more precautionary approach.

The evidence demonstrates a clear positive relationship between GDP growth and our environmental crisis. In addition, there are no known solutions that can be employed to continue to support economic growth and sufficiently address this crisis. Therefore, is it moral to rely on unproven or non-existent technological fixes? When leading scientists agree on the drivers of these crises, why do our political leaders knowingly allow these drivers to continue?

Throughout human history those in power attempt to retain power. This has been called "elite rigidity" (Geyer and Rihani 2012) or "social reproduction" (Wright 2010). In many ways our current political system is currently rigid and unchanging in order to protect the individuals and corporations who benefit most from the current fossil fuel-based, profit-maximizing system (Klein 2015). This is one reason the US has been demoted to the status of a "flawed democracy" (Economist Intelligence Unit 2019). Green growth is an ideology promoted to protect the current system and conceal the underlying contradictions leading us further into environmental crises (Gunderson et al. 2018c). However, is it moral to protect the economic interests of the few, through promoting false solutions, while putting all people, ecosystems, and other species at risk? Youth environmental activists increasingly demand that world leaders protect their future and "put people before profits," drawing attention to the immorality of continuing with business as usual. The fact that the current system is unable to respond to a moral imperative that resonates with nearly all humans reveals the need to radically change the system.

The ongoing failure to address our environmental crisis contributes to multiple forms of injustice. Failing to provide a safe climate and environment for future generations of humans results in generational injustice. Causing widespread species extinction and population collapse is an issue of interspecies injustice and ecocide. In addition, those who are and will continue to be most impacted by these crises are primarily poor people in the Global South, or the "global majority." Our environmental crisis will increasingly be experienced unequally, hurting those who are most vulnerable. Yet it is wealthy countries who are most responsible for this crisis, who continue to overproduce and overconsume resources, and who need to do the most to urgently change course. As global injustices multiply, false solutions need to be exposed for what they are: unsubstantiated faith in technological solutions and green growth pathways that protect the current system and benefit the economic interests of the few.

Beyond economic growth

As stated by Hickel and Kallis (2019: 15), "policy should be made on the basis of robust empirical evidence, rather than on the basis of speculative theoretical possibilities." The evidence presented in this chapter makes a strong case that adhering to policies prioritizing economic growth not only limits the effectiveness of mitigation measures but ultimately undermines efforts to sufficiently address our environmental crisis. Relationships between GDP growth and increasing carbon emissions and biodiversity loss are clear and there is ample evidence that reducing overall material and energy consumption in wealthy countries would increase the success of efforts to address the climate and biodiversity crises.

Models and projections illustrate how reducing economic growth even slightly increases possible decoupling and emissions reductions. As Hickel and Kallis (2019: 7) explain in terms of resource use, "[a]s the growth rate approaches zero, absolute decoupling becomes more feasible, and is likely to last longer." Lower rates of production and consumption (resulting in lower GDP), would also allow for more success in climate mitigation efforts. Yet to keep warming within 1.5°C or 2°C targets substantial reductions are necessary. Schroder and Storm (2018) find that emissions reduction to limit warming to 2°C can be only accomplished if economic growth is reduced to 0.45% annually. However, a 1.5°C target has not been shown to be possible without a degrowth scenario (Hickel and Kallis 2019). Grubler et al. (2018) and Van Vuuren et al. (2018) both not only contain scenarios of keeping temperatures within 2°C, but also rely on reducing material and energy throughput. Lastly, Hickel (2019a) cites additional scenarios that illustrate the feasibility of reaching environmental targets and increasing social well-being with degrowth pathways (i.e., D'Allessandro et al. 2018; Victor 2019).

Given the evidence undermining the reality of effective and fast green growth, we need to rethink economic growth. As stated clearly by Hickel and Kallis (2019:15), "[i]t is more plausible that we will be able to achieve the necessary reductions in resource use and emissions without growth than with growth." Parrique et al. (2019: 59) similarly argue that in contrast to unproven negative emissions technologies and green growth strategies, "reducing production and consumption is not an abstract narrative." We know that the necessary reductions are possible and even desirable. Ecological economists and others argue that letting go of economic growth as a priority will allow space for other types of growth to flourish, increasing health, happiness, and environmental (and therefore human) sustainability (Daly 2013; Stiglitz 2019a,b).

4 The degrowth alternative

Given the mounting evidence that our current system is in crisis, and more specifically that never-ending economic growth is an unrealistic and dangerous goal, degrowth is receiving increasing levels of attention. Even if the current system were not in a state of crisis, many people would still be looking for alternatives that result in increased equality, well-being, quality of life, and environmental protection. Degrowth offers an alternative with the potential to help address our environmental crisis and increase social justice and well-being. In many ways degrowth is utopian, yet as Martinez-Alier (1992) explains, it is a concrete utopia: degrowth is scientifically informed and possible. Degrowth is not only possible, but the principles, practices, and policies to create a degrowth society already exist, although many in embryonic form. Here we describe degrowth, focusing on what a degrowth transition might entail and the potential for this transformation to justly address the climate and biodiversity crises.

Giorgos Kallis (2017: 10), one of degrowth's most vocal advocates, defines degrowth as "an equitable down-scaling of production and consumption that increases human well-being and enhances environmental conditions." Since planetary limits are being surpassed by over-developed or over-consuming wealthy nations, degrowth entails reduced material and energy throughput in these economies to a steady state of "enough" or sufficiency, while at the same time helping nations in the Global South to more sustainably achieve an improved quality of life (Kallis 2017). The overall goal of degrowth is not to reduce GDP; however, the changes required to reduce total material and energy throughput would result in a contraction of the economy and a reduction in GDP (Hickel 2019a). Yet, degrowth is not the same as a recession: the degrowth "hypothesis" posits that well-being and quality of life can improve even as total material and energy throughput decreases (Kallis 2018). The underlying goal is to equitably reduce total resource and energy use to a sustainable level that provides enough for everyone and correct for the current level of "overshoot" causing our environmental crisis.

Degrowth is not a new concept. It is widely described as having emerged from a question posed by Andre Gorz in the early 1970s (Kallis 2015a; Paulson 2017). Kallis' book *Degrowth* (2018) includes a detailed history of the evolution of degrowth. We will not repeat this history here, but it should be noted that key contributors to degrowth development include Nicholas Georgescsu-Roegen, Serge Latouche, and Joan Martinez-Alier as well as Herman Daly, Tim Jackson, and Peter Victor. Barcelona, Spain, has emerged as the epicenter for current degrowth research, education, and activism: the Autonomous University of Barcelona is home to prominent degrowth scholars and now offers a graduate program in degrowth. In addition, the academic collective "Research & Degrowth" coordinates networking among degrowth scholars and activists and an international degrowth conference is held at least every other year.

Beyond the definitions of degrowth, there are also specific visions, goals, and principles that are commonly articulated in the degrowth literature. We review several here. The first relates to the concept of embeddedness. As noted long ago by Karl Polanyi (2001 [1944]: 60), "Instead of economy being embedded in social relations, social relations are embedded in the economic system." Polanyi argued it should be the other way around. Kaup (2015) extends this notion further arguing that the economy needs to be re-embedded in both the social and natural spheres. Rather than society and nature being subject to economic rationale, to avoid social-ecological collapse, we must make economic goals subordinate to social and ecological well-being (Van Griethuysen 2010). Kallis (2018) as well as Demaria et al. (2019: 432) link the concept of embeddedness directly to degrowth, explaining that the purpose of degrowth is "to open up the opportunity for dis-embedding life from the totalizing effects of current economic structures and processes." Degrowth thus entails radical repriorization that opposes the supremacy of economic growth. To stay within ecological limits, the economy must be subordinate to and embedded within society and the environment/natural sphere (Figure 4.1).

Additional key functions, agendas, and principles related to degrowth have also been identified in the literature. Kallis (2015a) describes how in addition to a critique of growth, degrowth is also a slogan, a "missile word" (see Chapter 5), a theory, a policy, a way of life, and a social movement. Gabriel and Bond (2019: 328) list three primary agendas of degrowth: (1) to decrease material and energy

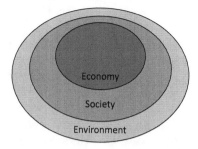

Figure 4.1 A nested depiction of sustainability from ecological economics that illustrates the economy embedded within society and the environment.

Source: https://en.wikipedia.org/wiki/File:Nested_sustainability-v2.gif.

throughput, (2) to emphasize social justice, well-being, and inclusion, and (3) to create voluntary democratic channels to participate in decision-making. Jarvis (2019: 7) states that "a degrowth perspective can be identified in the literature with respect to four transformations: extending human relations instead of market relations; deepening democracy; defending ecosystems; and realizing a more equal global distribution of wealth." Lastly, Kallis (2018) emphasizes several key principles of degrowth: reducing throughput, equality, democracy, re-localization, diversifying economic forms, decommodification, care, sharing, building relationships, conviviality, and celebration.

Many scholars have debated at what scale a degrowth transition should take place. Most degrowth scholars agree that individual level changes, while important for illustrating how individuals can live sufficiently and consume less energy and material resources, are not enough to transform society towards a degrowth economy. In that case, does degrowth require a community level, bottom-up, grass-roots-based transition? Or does it require a state-led, top-down, policy-driven transition? In accord with other theories of social change (Wright 2010; Kallis 2018; Wright 2019), we do not believe a degrowth transition fits into this "either-or" line of thinking. Here, we examine what degrowth could entail at (1) the community level, (2) with regards to work, and (3) in terms of government interventions and policies. It should be noted that institutions at different scales can either support or constrain a degrowth transition, therefore simultaneous and reinforcing transformations are necessary at multiple scales of influence. In our communities, workplaces, and government policies, we need to create "the institutions that will allow us to live with enough" (Kallis and March 2015: 8). We acknowledge that a plurality of degrowth visions exist and what we describe here is only one of many possibilities.

Degrowth in households and communities

Many degrowth scholars and activists have written about what degrowth living looks like. This includes working fewer hours, repairing items rather than replacing them, increased home provisioning, participating in low-energy leisure activities (e.g., playing piano), using low-energy transportation methods (e.g., biking or walking), and using more low-energy strategies to take care of personal needs and household chores (e.g., line-drying clothing). Alexander and Yacoumis (2018) estimate that through these types of changes total household energy consumption can be reduced by 49%. These descriptions and analyses provide necessary examples of how people could live in a degrowth world. Yet alone, individual changes are unlikely to result in a degrowth transition, as institutions at larger scales restrict what is possible. Still it is important to understand how lifestyles can be changed in-line with degrowth principles.

At the community-level, examples of degrowth living include enterprises that increase local production, offer alternative economic options, increase sharing, and encourage cooperative and common use of resources (Kallis et al. 2012; Bloemmen et al. 2015; Kunze and Becker 2015; Jarvis 2018). Local production includes community gardens and community-supported agriculture. Alternative economic options include barter markets, the use of local currency, and time banking. Sharing can be supported through neighborhood book sharing, tool sharing, and ride/car sharing. Collective ownership and management of land, energy systems, and housing can increase shared use and democratic participation. Examples of these endeavors can be found across the globe as an increasing number of families and communities are participating in "nowtopias," experimenting with degrowth living (Demaria et al. 2019). While there are many ways to encourage degrowth living, below we highlight three specific areas for ground-up or "grass-roots" community transformation: (1) shifting culture and values, (2) fostering sharing of spaces and resources, and (3) (re)commoning resources and energy.

Degrowth living requires a shift away from consumer culture and towards a culture of sufficiency where quality is valued over quantity and new forms of abundance emerge. This cultural transition is in line with what Juliet Schor (2010) calls *Plentitude* and involves simple living, yet feeling satisfied with enough rather than always wanting more. Degrowth involves a cultural and paradigmatic shift where collective social and ecological values are placed before personal wealth accumulation (Brossman and Islar 2019). It also involves fostering a "culture of self-limitation" that, in contrast to austerity, is chosen through self-awareness and ethical rationale: "social needs are constructed and can be deliberated on, negotiated, regulated or limited" (Kallis 2019: 270). In this way degrowth blurs and reshapes cultural norms and values into forms that are more relevant and appropriate for addressing our environmental crisis (Perkins 2019). This cultural shift would be reinforced and encouraged through other changes such as advertising restrictions (discussed later) and public campaigns promoting these values, such as those that spurred consumption changes among the US households during World War II.

Part of this cultural shift involves valuing sharing over personal ownership, as sharing can both reduce environmental impacts and increase human connectedness. While many people talk about "sharing economies" (e.g., Airbnb or Uber), in many cases these alternatives remain focused on individualism, profit, and valuing things before relationships. In contrast, the sharing of spaces or the sequential sharing of resources or tools can build relationships. Shared housing through cooperatives, co-housing, or eco-villages provides many opportunities for sharing space and resources, reducing environmental impacts. As Jarvis (2019: 258) explains,

> neoliberal market economies, notably in the UK, USA and Australia, typically sponsor a dominant housing regime (owner occupation) that locks the respective society into a homogeneous material culture that inhibits sharing. This coincides with negative consequences for the planet, including extraordinarily high carbon emissions and energy consumption associated with conventional single-family dwelling.

In contrast if we cast aside economic growth and hyper-individualism (which promotes excessive personal consumption and fuels economic growth), then sharing material resources, housing, and spaces allows for reducing environmental impacts and increasing social connectedness. Jarvis (2019: 257) states that sharing in line with degrowth principles involves prioritizing "intentional 'we' thinking and ethical purpose" instead of the "cultural norms, such as hyper-individual dwelling and conspicuous consumption." Because the growth imperative relies on the private ownership and control of production (and this drives competition), addressing ownership and control is especially important to intentionally contract total material and energy use.

To enhance sharing, access to resources, and reduce environmental impacts, collective ownership and the (re)commoning of spaces, resources, and energy is key. The commons have received significant attention since Ostrom's book *Governing the Commons* (1990), which established that Hardin's (1968) "tragedy of the commons" is by no means universal. Bollier (2014: 15) defines commons as "paradigms that combine a distinct community with a set of social practice, values and norms that are used to manage a resource." While a resource can be a commons, "communing" is a social process of collaborative stewardship over shared resources that builds connection and community (Helfrich and Bollier 2015). Commons are not only a resource but also a means by which people work collectively to use a resource for the benefit of all. While the global market economy grew from enclosing commons, degrowth reverses this trend. Increasing common resources allows more access for everyone and may even be required for sufficiency without economic growth (Hickel 2019a, 2019b). In addition, Perkins (2019: 185): explains: "(Re)commoning opens an ethical, political, and currently relevant means to motivate and cushion degrowth, broaden its appeal, and emphasize its practical/livelihood applications."

In terms of climate change mitigation, the (re)commoning of energy and the development of community-renewable energy systems can be an important step in a degrowth transition (Gunderson et al. 2018b). We agree with Byrne and others (2009: 90) that:

> although commons institutions do not in and of themselves guarantee eradication of environmentally exploitive practices, they do offer elements for recovery of political agency in the formation of choices regarding energy and environmental futures and the foundation for a normative reconstitution of the good life.

In addition, the Mercator Research Institute on Global Commons (2017) argues that energy should be a common good as it is essential for human well-being and is often underprovided. Energy use affects the global commons through carbon emissions and climate change. Treating energy as a common could help facilitate a transition to renewable energy and also to reduce overall energy consumption through just and democratic means.

While we have focused on degrowth living at the household and community level in this section, we agree with Kallis (2018) that these "grassroots" practices are alone insufficient for a degrowth transition. They are important because they illustrate what degrowth living looks like and the range of social benefits, and because "they represent and nourish alternative value systems that are in tension with the dominant value form" (Kallis 2018: 136). However, they are insufficient as they do not address the power relations and social structures that reinforce the supremacy of economic growth. We agree that building alternative models in the "cracks" of the current system is important, but more is necessary (Wright 2010). While local actions alone are not enough to address our environmental crisis, they demonstrate alternative models of living that are both possible and worth pursuing.

Degrowth and work

Changes in work aligned with degrowth principles are critical for a degrowth transition and can also stimulate or allow for community and national level degrowth initiatives. Work is a central locus for transformation, as work is where decisions are made about increasing rates of production and the advertising used to sell more and more goods to consumers. Degrowth would eliminate the automatic reinvestment of surplus value into further production and instead open up channels for other decisions about the allocation of surplus (Barca 2019). Keynes predicted in 1930 that, due to increases in productivity, by 2030 people would only work 15 hours to support their material needs; but instead these gains have been used to increase production and profits for the few (Hickel 2019a). Most workers remain powerless, alienated, and overworked without time for family, creativity, and human flourishing. Two specific changes in work are central to a degrowth transition: (1) workplace democracy and (2) reduced working hours.

Democracy in the workplace or "economic democracy" is critical for addressing worker alienation and opening up opportunities to use productivity gains in ways other than expansion and increasing levels of production. As explained by Barca (2019), degrowth should involve worker-controlled democratic production systems where alienation is addressed through collective ownership of the products of labor and democratic deliberation about the best use of surplus. Barca (2019) states that "the project of building a degrowth society can only start from fostering dealienation by reopening the possibility for workers control and economic democracy, from the workplace to society at large." Khmara and Kronenberg (2018) discuss how degrowth principles could shape new business goals and argues that it would entail an alternative culture of business, values created collaboratively, democratic decision-making, reducing environmental impacts, and making products that are high quality, long-lived, and repairable.

Models of economic democracy already exist and include worker control of privately-owned firms, worker control of publicly owned firms, and worker control of worker-owned firms (e.g., worker-owned cooperatives). Worker decision-making power ranges from workers receiving a notification that a decision is being made to a majority representation in the forum or body that makes decisions (Schweickart 1992; Archer 1995; Boillat et al. 2012). There are also hybrid models, such as requiring worker representation on a firm's board of directors. In a democratic system, workers would directly participate in decision-making or have elected representatives participate in all decisions that have impacts on workers and the future of the firm. This includes schedules, work speed, allocation of work duties, technologies and tools used, hiring and firing employees, product quality and quantity, profit-distribution, and investment (Schweickart 1992).

While there is nothing inherent in the structure of economic democracy that necessitates reduced throughput, it is widely agreed that democracy in the workplace is a prerequisite to opening up more opportunities for changes in production systems. Degrowth thinkers support economic democracy largely because it can create conditions favorable to new priorities that allow for the shrinking of throughput in a socially just way (e.g., Boillat et al. 2012; Johanisova and Wolf 2012). Economic democracy would allow for reduced environmental impacts through allowing investment decisions to be collective rather than solely for private gain, by moving beyond requirements to advertise and sell more product, and through allowing people to be involved in decisions that impact their lives and the environment (Boillat et al. 2012). Bayon (2015: 191) also argues that "[i]f work were under the control of workers, human work would be much more likely to be environmentally friendly."

In addition to democratizing work, work time reduction (WTR) is critical to support a degrowth transition (Kallis 2018; Gunderson 2019). WTR would involve reducing annual working hours to a new standard, without decreases in pay or loss of benefits, and would likely also involve work-sharing models. Work sharing allows fewer hours worked while avoiding unemployment (Schor 2015). As explained by Pullinger (2014:14) there are multiple avenues for WTR including limiting the number of working hours per week, increasing holidays each year, increasing time for maternity and paternity leave, increasing sick leave, and offering pre-retirement transitions. Examples of WTR already exist. Most examples have been temporary policies during economic downturns, but increasingly WTR is occurring in European countries (LaJeunesse 2009). As we will detail below, there are both social and environmental benefits associated with WTR.

In terms of social benefits, WTR can help to increase levels of full employment, address alienated labor, improve quality of life, and enhance human flourishing. Heikkurinen et al. (2019) explain the benefits related to increased employment and addressing alienated labor: The generalized reduction of working time amounts to a choice as to the kind of society we wish to live in. This can be seen from its two inseparable objectives: (a) that everyone should work less, so that everyone may work and may also develop outside their working lives the personal potential which cannot find expression in their work; (b) that a much greater proportion of the population should be able to have access to skilled, complex, creative, and responsible occupational activities which allow them continually to develop and grow.

Hickel (2019a: 65) further explains how WTR would enhance well-being:

> People would be able to work less without any loss to their quality of life, thus producing less unnecessary stuff and therefore generating less pressure for unnecessary consumption. Meanwhile, with more free time people would be able to have fun, enjoy conviviality with loved ones, cooperate with neighbors, care for friends and relatives, cook healthy food, exercise and enjoy nature, thus rendering unnecessary the patterns of consumption that are driven by time scarcity.

Other social benefits include time to do creative work, gardening, and self-provisioning including canning and processing home-grown foods, sewing, knitting, art, and pottery.

In terms of environmental benefits, WTR has been shown to reduce carbon emissions and ecological footprints (Knight et al. 2013). Shorter working hours involve lower rates of production and reduce pressure on resource and energy use. WTR can result in reduced total energy use, as working hours are associated with energy consumption (Fitzgerald et al. 2015). Rosnick and Weisbrot (2006) estimate that if working hours were reduced instead of using productivity gains for increased production, the US would consume 20% less energy. Rosnick (2013: 124) also posits that if we reduce working hours 0.5% annually over the next century we can "eliminate about one-quarter to one-half, if not more, of any warming that is not already locked in." In general, because longer working hours are associated with increased carbon emissions, ecological footprints, and energy use, WTR represents a potentially powerful climate change mitigation strategy.

However, WTR does not necessarily guarantee less environmental impacts because leisure could conceivably be spent doing more environmentally harmful activities like shopping or travel (Knight et al. 2013; Gunderson 2019). Therefore, changes in culture and values (described above) as well as in advertising (described below) would also be important to encourage low-impact activities. However, with economic democracy and WTR there would likely be more diverse goals, less marketing and advertising, and less pressure on individuals to consume unnecessary goods. More free-time also allows for the self-provisioning activities mentioned above that are low-impact but do take more time than purchasing pre-made products.

Organized labor is historically responsible for WTR and many labor unions have increasingly attempted to combine labor and environmental goals (Gunderson 2019). In Europe, where working time is around 35 hours a week, labor unions have recently demanded WTR. For example, the German metal worker union demanded and were granted a 28-hour work week for up to two years in 2018 (Bulman 2018). Labor unions in the UK have also fought for WTR, including the Royal Mail workers (Harper 2017). As environmental concerns increase, if labor movements add the environment to their rationale for demanding WTR they may have even more success. In this way, WTR helps to address the widely depicted but false antagonism between jobs and the environment (see Goodstein 1999). Job guarantees, as laid out in the Green New Deal (HR 109), also could help to alleviate this tension and provide necessary support for workers during an energy transition. Incorporating WTR and work-sharing would increase possible social and environmental benefits. However, policies at the federal level are required to standardize WTR and to allow for the full range social and environmental benefits.

National and global policies for degrowth

National and global level policies are necessary for a degrowth transition and scholars and activists have already outlined a number of key proposals. As described by Schmid (2019), there are platforms for both moderate and a radical degrowth visions: moderate degrowth retains much of the market-based and state institutions in their current form while radical degrowth questions these institutions and focuses more on community-based initiatives emphasizing environmental and social justice. However, as we will discuss further in the next chapter, some seemingly moderate proposals may serve as "non-reformist reforms" (Gorz 1967): reforms that once implemented reshape what is possible moving forward and open up opportunities for more radical transformation (Kallis 2018).

Some policies directly relate to supporting the changes described in the previous sections. For example, policies would be necessary to standardize WTR and to ensure that transitions are equitable and just. Universal basic income could also be used as a social support to reduce vulnerability during transition, and expanding access to free healthcare, education, and public transportation could increase well-being without individuals needing higher incomes (Hickel 2019a). Policies could also support, incentivize, or subsidize cooperative work governance and ownership as well as common resource management. New forms of public housing could emphasize low-carbon living and be designed to maximize opportunities for sharing resources, tools, and services such as childcare and elder care. While there are many policy proposals in the degrowth literature, here we review selected proposals that evidence suggests would have a profound impact on alleviating environmental stressors: (1) advertising restrictions, (2) a wealth tax or income cap, (3) abolishing GDP as an indicator of progress, (4) nationalizing and decommissioning the fossil fuel industry, and (5) creating a global democratic "cap-and-share" program to radically and justly reduce carbon emissions.

Advertising restrictions are critical for reducing overconsumption. Galbraith (1958) long ago identified how advertising plays a key role in creating the desires that fuel consumption. Advertising and the media are used to create "false needs" through manipulation (Marcuse 1964). Debord (1983) called them "pseudo-needs" created specifically to maintain the growing economy. Advertising influences individuals' perceptions of themselves and their social status, compelling them to buy products to address manufactured dissatisfaction (Horkheimer and Adorno 1969). Buying alternatives and "voting with your dollar" supports a belief that through different purchasing one can alleviate negative impacts, yet still fuels over-consumption. Total US expenditures on advertising have increased to over $205 billion annually (Griner 2017). While restricting advertising seems "un-American," even in the US, advertisements aimed at children were banned until 1984 (Molotsky 1988). Banning advertising for harmful or status commodities could significantly help reduce overconsumption. Other restrictions could include banning advertising in public spaces (Hickel 2019a). Advertising restrictions complement other proposals discussed above: democracy in the workplace would likely reduce the imperative to advertise, and reduced advertising would help ensure that increased free-time due to WTR did not result in increased levels of consumption.

Addressing inequality while reducing overconsumption is a key goal of degrowth and involves the redistribution of wealth (Hickel 2019a). This would reduce environmental harm, as wealthy individuals have a much higher environmental impact. For example, according to Chancel and Piketty (2015) those in the top 1% income bracket in the US emit over 300 metric tons of carbon dioxide equivalent per capita compared to 20 metric tons for the average North American and well above the 6.2 global average. Due to the extreme level of current inequality, ensuring that human needs and social goals can be met without growth will require that wealth is more fairly distributed (Hickel 2019a). Therefore, a wealth tax, income cap, or other redistributive reform (see Buch-Hansen and Koch 2019) is critical in terms of equity and to reduce the excessive resource and energy use driving our climate and biodiversity crises. In addition, other tax reforms could discourage general overconsumption of unnecessary goods. For example, taxes can be placed on luxury goods; the square-footage of large homes; and the carbon emissions associated with goods, services, and transportation. Last, taxes could be used to support a universal basic income that offers a social safety-net during transition.

Reducing material and energy throughput will remain elusive until GDP growth is abandoned as a social goal. The call to abolish GDP as an indicator of progress is coming not only from supporters of degrowth but from an increasing number of scholars, economists, and pundits. As explained by Nobel award-winning economist Joseph Stiglitz (2019b): "[i]f we measure the wrong thing, we will do the wrong thing" and currently what we are measuring and prioritizing is leading us further into a global crisis. GDP has also failed to be a good indicator of well-being and quality of life (O'Neill 2012; Stiglitz 2019a,b). Alternative indicators, including the Index of Sustainable Economic Welfare, Gross National Happiness, and the General Progress Indicator, illustrate that GDP remains a poor indicator of social progress in terms of health, education, well-being, and happiness. Given the original purpose of GDP, and the abundant evidence that increasing GDP is leading us further into crisis, there remains no ethical justification for continuing to prioritize GDP growth. While some maintain that GDP should still be used as one of many indicators, others argue that it should be abolished altogether and replaced with indicators that are more appropriate.

Addressing the climate and biodiversity crises will necessarily involve phasing out the use of fossil fuels. As discussed in Chapter 2, increases in energy efficiency and renewable energy sources are not reducing fossil fuel use. Without government intervention, it is highly unlikely that fossil fuel companies will stop further exploration and extraction. A first step is to end all subsidies for fossil fuels. In addition, governments can nationalizing fossil fuel companies and end further extraction. The Next Systems Project (2020) details multiple policy proposals to nationalize the industry. This could include actions similar to the 2008 financial crisis response: creating new money ("quantitative easing"), but instead of bailing out banks, using the money to buyout fossil fuel companies (Skandier 2018). They argue that government buyouts are not uncommon and have occurred throughout US history, including the buyout of tobacco companies between 2004 and 2014. Gowan (2018) also proposes nationalizing fossil fuel companies, which he states has already been proposed in the United Kingdom and is taking place in Norway. He explains that according to US takings laws, governments can purchase fossil fuel companies at market value. Gowan (2018) states that purchasing 51% of fossil fuel shares (a majority stake) would cost about $410 billion and argues that this cost is small compared to the long-term costs of the climate crisis.

Last, to effectively mitigate climate change, global-level climate governance is necessary that focuses on justly and rapidly reducing carbon emissions. Although carbon sequestration through reforestation, afforestation, and restoration efforts can play a role in mitigation and should also be pursued for conservation purposes, carbon sequestration approaches alone will not be enough to avoid 1.5°C or 2°C warming (Stuart et al. 2020). Emissions reduction must be done quickly, effectively, and equitably. Kallis (2018) argues for a global climate agreement involving a "cap and share" model: a total limit (cap) for global emissions would be divided equitably and reduced over time. Any creation of a global "cap and share" program will require democratic participation to ensure that allocations of allowable emissions are just. Gunderson (2018) examines possibilities for global environmental governance and argues that participatory and deliberative approaches have been successful at smaller scales and represent a promising model for global climate governance. Equitable representation is key and citizens from vulnerable regions, especially in the Global South, should play a primary role in deliberations. While many challenges currently constrain the realization of such global initiatives, it is still important to identify these desirable governance possibilities.

From critique to vision

Degrowth represents a critique of the economic growth imperative and a call to redesign social systems to stay within ecological limits while improving social well-being. This book has devoted significant attention to articulating this critique, illustrating how the current growth propelled system will inhibit efforts to stave off the negative impacts of the climate and biodiversity crises. Recent publications provide evidence to support a compelling case for this critique, which justifies changing our social priorities and the institutions that support these priorities. While evidence and data strongly support this critique, the more difficult challenge remains identifying the alternatives that will provide the best path forward.

Moving beyond the critique component of degrowth is difficult due to the challenge of identifying policies and programs that in different conditions would result in the best social and ecological outcomes. Degrowth scholars and activists have identified many different visions of what the degrowth alternatives could entail. Here, we have highlighted only one possible vision. However, which paths will result in the best possible social and ecological outcomes remains unknown, and indeed *all* face significant obstacles. Yet thinking about, planning, and designing these possible and desirable futures is essential. When conditions ripen for change, it is those who already have a concrete vision who are ready to lead the way.

5   Questions and critiques

Degrowth proposals have resulted in widespread debates, controversies, and critiques. This is not surprising, as degrowth questions the growth imperative: a goal that has shaped government policies and social organization explicitly for decades and implicitly for longer. It is still widely assumed that growth is good and it will take time to counter this myth with the alternative narrative: more and more growth, past the point of sufficiency, is harmful and is threatening the biosphere we all depend on.

Degrowth is still widely misunderstood as simply a decrease in GDP and therefore misinterpreted as recession. However, degrowth is a planned social transformation to reduce material and energy throughput and stay within ecological limits. While there are many questions, debates, and critiques related to degrowth (see Kallis 2018), here we focus on three: (1) if degrowth is compatible with capitalism or socialism, (2) how degrowth might impact the Global South, and (3) if the term "degrowth" is best for building a social movement.

Degrowth, capitalism, and socialism

Scholars have long argued about the compatibility between degrowth, capitalism, and socialism. First, it is critical to acknowledge that both lay and scholarly definitions of capitalism and socialism vary widely and both concepts are usually either commonly misinterpreted or depicted as ideal types. While seen as absolutes and opposites, in most societies examples of socialism and capitalism exist simultaneously in what Wright (2019) describes as an ecosystem of economic relations. Although some relations do dominate and largely preclude other possibilities. Because capitalism and socialism are so widely misunderstood, many scholars, pundits, and politicians now question the usefulness of these terms and some suggest abandoning them altogether. Here we

recognize the challenges in using these terms yet will attempt to artic-
ulate what they mean and how they relate to degrowth.

Whether degrowth is compatible with capitalism depends on how
one defines capitalism. If capitalism is an economic system where
there is private property, markets to distribute goods, and money used
as a basis of exchange; then they are compatible. However, degrowth
would likely increase the sharing of goods and alternative/local cur-
rencies. If one defines capitalism as an economic system that continually accumulates capital for the sake of more capital accumulation,
then degrowth is not compatible with capitalism. While in some cases
what capitalism is remains contested, there is agreement among many
scholars and activists that the defining feature of capitalism is its dependency on never-ending growth in production, consumption, and
profit accumulation. In other words, modern capitalism is a system of
ever-expanding accumulation, which drives economic growth (Wallerstein 1979; Kallis 2018).

In a capitalist enterprise with the imperative to maximize profits,
surplus must be reinvested to increase production. This propels forward production and the advertising necessary to sell products whether
they increase well-being or not and whether they cause environmental
destruction or not. Firms are compelled to adhere to this model due
to the realities of debt, competition, and investment that drive forward
the engines of production. This system also incentivizes externaliz-
ing environmental damage and paying workers the lowest acceptable
wages. Even a business owner with concerns about the environment
and worker well-being faces significant obstacles prioritizing these
concerns while staying competitive in a system that prioritizes profit.

These capitalist relations have been described as a "treadmill of
production" that depends on ever increasing levels of consumption to
keep going (Schnaiberg 1980). The modern version of this process is
explained particularly well by Jason Hickel, an anthropologist who
remains a vocal critic of economic growth (Hickel 2019a: 62):

> Industrialists who fear that people's existing needs are too limited
> to absorb capitalism's immense productive output must seek to
> create new needs, or else the juggernaut will grind to a halt. This is
> accomplished by various means. One is to expand desires through
> sophisticated advertising campaigns – and to extend these cam-
> paigns into all public and private spaces – manipulating people's
> emotions and psychology to create new "needs" for products that
> promise to grant them a sense of self-esteem, status, identity,
> sexual prowess and so on that did not exist before and indeed do

not have to exist. Another is to create products that are designed to break down quickly (like laptops and smart phones today) or become rapidly obsolete (as with the rise of throwaway fashion), and which therefore must be replaced more frequently than would otherwise be necessary. Another is to preclude the development of public goods in order to ensure that people have no choice but to purchase private alternatives: for instance, blocking the construction of effective public transportation systems in order to ensure a steady stream of demand for the automobile industry.

The capitalist system must find ways to keep increasing the levels of production and must also create new ways to sell more and more products. Yet, is this system rational in a world with finite resources and accelerating rates of global warming and biodiversity loss?

Degrowth represents a confrontation and critique of capitalism because it directly challenges the prioritization of profits, the "treadmill of production," and the economic growth imperative. As explained by Gómez-Baggethun (2020: 5): "By favoring redistribution over expansion, the degrowth utopia represents a frontal attack on the core ideology of modern industrial capitalism." To keep the treadmill going, capitalist systems also create notions of "limitless needs" and "eternal scarcity" to justify ongoing expansion and increasing levels of production (Kallis 2019: 270). Citizens have been purposefully turned into super-consumers to keep the treadmill going. Degrowth challenges the treadmill and instead prioritizes social and ecological well-being. In these ways degrowth is incompatible with capitalism. However, it should be noted that not all degrowth supporters agree. For example, some degrowth scholars have evaded confronting capitalism either to avoid the stigma associated with being "anti-capitalist" or to avoid a hegemonic depiction of capitalism that might undermine possibilities for community-based degrowth projects (see Schmid 2019).

It is the capitalist system that drives our environmental crisis and also prevents proposed solutions from being effective. This creates two contradictions. First, is the capital-climate contradiction: the contradictory needs of capital to continually expand, on the one hand, and the destructive climatic (and ecological) impacts of this expansion despite the need for a relatively stable climate system, on the other. This contradiction is a global-level illustration of what O'Connor (1998) calls the "second contradiction of capitalism," where capitalism degrades its own conditions of production (see also Weis 2010; Harvey 2014; Wright and Nyberg 2015). A related contradiction is the technical potential-productive relations contradiction: the existence of technologies (e.g., wind and solar energy systems) that could be used to rapidly reduce emissions in different social conditions, on the one hand, and the "fettering" by the structural barriers of capitalist social relations, on the other (for more detail on these two contradictions, see Gunderson et al. 2018a). The false solutions outlined in Chapter 2 will continually fail to meet their goals because they mask or simply ignore these contradictions rather than address them.

Whether one is a critic of capitalist systems in general or focuses only on the economic growth imperative, solutions that fail to address economic growth also fail to get at the root driver of the climate and biodiversity crises. In addition to confronting the priorities, institutions, and relations that define modern capitalism, degrowth also challenges the culture of capitalism. As explained by Kallis (2015c: 1): "[d]egrowth challenges not only the outcomes, but the very spirit of capitalism. Capitalism knows no limits, it only knows how to expand, creating while destroying." Degrowth values and principles challenge consumerism, individualism, and greed and instead focus on sufficiency, sharing, common resources, relationships, conviviality, and care (Kallis 2018). In addition, rather than supporting a culture of always needing more (largely propelled by advertising), degrowth promotes a "culture of self-limitation" that values restraint to enhance social and ecological well-being (Kallis 2019: 270). In all of these ways, degrowth in theory and practice is incompatible with modern capitalism, which remains dependent on economic growth.

If degrowth is not compatible with capitalism, is it compatible with socialism? Again, we need to define what we mean by socialism. The idea of socialism emerged as an alternative to capitalism in response to the injustices related to worker exploitation and class power during the industrial revolution. While socialist ideals include equality, worker control over the means of production, and prioritizing the well-being of all, countries that attempted to adopt a "socialist" model largely resulted in authoritarian bureaucracies who prioritized economic growth at the expense of social justice and environmental protection. Wright (2010) calls these examples of "statism," because the means of production are owned almost exclusively by the state, and argues they are not true examples of socialism because they lack democracy, worker control of production, and the prioritization of well-being. While visions of a socialist society often involve prioritizing democracy, equality, and well-being, and, before Stalinism, had been defined as worker control of the means of production, most statist examples that have been called "socialist" adopted capitalist imperatives prioritizing profit and economic growth. In other words, the "actually existing" examples of so-called "socialism" are incompatible with degrowth.

In contrast, "democratic" socialism entails the democratization of work, prioritizing equality and well-being, a state that represents people through democratic processes, and democratic mechanisms to retain public control of industries. A form of socialism based on democracy, equality, and well-being leaves room for society to decide if growth should be prioritized. As explained by Kallis (2019: 267): "capitalism is geared to grow or die. Socialism could, at least in principle, secure a better quality of life with less resources and energy, and distribute them more equally." If we recognize the dependency of capitalism on perpetual economic growth, then a true alternative to capitalism would also need to cast off the growth imperative. Gorz argued that unless we have "equality without growth" then socialism is merely a "continuation of capitalism by other means" (cited in Kallis 2015a). Marcuse (1967: 3) also explained that "even Marx was still too tied to the notion of a continuum of progress, that even his idea of socialism may not yet represent, or no longer represent, the determinate negation of capitalism it was supposed to." If socialism is a true negation of capitalism, it must also negate perpetual economic growth. Degrowth would only be compatible with a form of democratic socialism without growth.

Eco-socialism acknowledges ecological relationships, focuses on the environmental degradation caused by capitalism, and, in many ways, complements degrowth. Eco-socialism emphasizes environmental protection in addition to the socialist goals of equality, democracy, and well-being. Löwy (2006) describes eco-socialism based on democratic ecological planning "putting human and planetary needs first and foremost" and for a new economy based on use-value and need rather than exchange value and profit. Foster (2010: 16) argues that the social and ecological are inseparable and describes the key elements of eco-socialism as:

> (1) social use, not ownership, of nature; (2) rational regulation by the associated producers of the metabolic relation between humanity and nature; and (3) satisfaction of communal needs—not only of present but also future generations (and life itself)

With this inclusion of nature and sustainability, eco-socialism supports many of the same goals and ideas as degrowth. Baer (2019) specifically describes "democratic eco-socialism" as recognizing that we live on a finite planet with ecological limits and rejecting the prioritization of economic growth in order to protect future generations.

While eco-socialism and degrowth evolved distinctively, in terms of embeddedness (see Chapter 4), they both aim to subordinate the economy to social and ecological goals and we believe that to accomplish this goal key elements from both degrowth and eco-socialism are necessary. First, eco-socialism must explicitly call for the downshifting of production and consumption and reject economic growth. As we have argued in this book, the eco-socialist goal of regulating the human-nature metabolism to protect life and future generations (Foster 2010) can only be achieved by reducing material and energy throughput and therefore abandoning economic growth. Second, degrowth needs to be a socialist project or an explicit rejection of capitalism. We agree with Clark, Foster, and York (2010) that "limits to growth" perspectives like degrowth must target the capitalist system rather than an abstract notion of growth. Like Kallis (2018), other degrowthers must acknowledge that challenging the growth imperative requires challenging capitalism. Despite debates and disagreements, degrowth and eco-socialism are largely complementary, and we encourage more collaboration and integration.

Degrowth and the global south

Many critics of degrowth have focused on its incompatibility with the development needs of poor people in the Global South, or more accurately the "global majority." There are three areas of concern we will address here. First, there is a common and false assumption that countries in the Global South would be forced to degrow. This comes from a lack of knowledge or a misunderstanding of degrowth. The second concern is that countries in the Global South could be adversely affected if wealthy countries pursue degrowth. This concern is warranted and deserves further consideration. Finally, we consider if degrowth could allow for more beneficial pathways of development. By challenging the Western development model based on economic growth, degrowth opens up possibilities for alternative development pathways that could be chosen by the people in the global majority rather than forced upon them.

Degrowth scholars agree that production and consumption should not be reduced in places where many people's needs are still not being met. For example, Demaria et al. (2019) argue that in cases where people are living with less than enough, there is clearly a need to increase production and consumption. Degrowth is "not a material process of lowering consumption, an irrelevant demand for those who live within conditions of poverty" (Demaira et al. 2019: 439). The authors also argue that poverty and "underdevelopment" are not a consequence of the absence of economic growth, yet in many cases are the consequences of economic growth and development interventions. In contrast to growth being seen as alleviating poverty, it should be recognized that in many ways growth has resulted in poverty. Recent analysis suggests that developing countries have been net-creditors to the Global North, sending money out a rate beyond the "aid" received from the developed world (Global Financial Integrity (GFI) 2016). Hickel (2017) details how the Western development model has been tremendously harmful to the global majority while being portrayed as helpful. In agreement, Demaria et al. (2019: 439) argue:

> The ideology of growth disguises continued colonial relations with a pretense of generalized betterment, while securing the unequal exchanges and the access by capital to cheap raw materials and human labour that is necessary for sustaining growth for some at the expense of others.

Meeting the needs of those in the Global South is critical, but the goal should not simply be economic growth, which Hickel (2017) illustrates goes largely to the few or is exported. A more appropriate goal is meeting the needs of people and supporting health and well-being. Growth to meet those needs could be done with the goal of sufficiency in mind, rather than the goal of never-ending economic growth. In other words, we must improve "the development model to make it more efficient at converting resources into well-being" (Hickel 2019c).

While a goal of degrowth is socio-ecological *global* justice, degrowth scholars do not yet fully understand or agree upon the likely impacts of degrowth in wealthy countries on the more vulnerable members of the global majority (Dengler and Seebacher 2019). One position is that degrowth in rich countries is essential to allow resources to be freed up and used in poor countries. Hickel (2019c) argues that it is necessary for rich countries to degrow in order to achieve a good life for all, otherwise the additional resource use in the Global South would further the overshoot of planetary boundaries. Kallis (2015b) explains how "strong carbon caps for the North and better terms of trade for the South can help compensate for past carbon and resource debts, redistributing wealth between North and South."

However, another possibility is that degrowth in places like the US, Northern Europe, and Australia could adversely impact the economy and workers in poor countries where most goods are now produced. In a highly globalized economy, care would have to be taken to avoid sudden adverse impacts to already vulnerable populations. In addition, Dengler and Seebacher (2019: 251) discuss how degrowth needs to avoid the neo-colonialism that results when the North (again) sets the global agenda; they argue that a

> feminist decolonial degrowth approach, which is sensitive to patriarchal gender relations, colonial continuities and economic structures that enable and (re-)produce these relations, can contribute to the endeavor of building North-South bridges at equal footing.

Degrowth scholars and activists are increasingly working to develop more of these North-South bridges and exploring how to pursue degrowth without imposing Northern ideas. Many agree that degrowth for the Global South should represent an attempt to undo the imposition of Western ideas that have furthered colonialism and inequality (e.g., Demaria et al. 2019).

If pursued with these considerations in mind, some degrowth scholars argue that degrowth can open up alternative pathways for development in the Global South that could result in more beneficial outcomes for all. Challenging the growth paradigm also challenges the model of Western development which imposes economic growth as a priority. Yet, what if countries in the Global South could achieve high(er) levels of well-being on a different path? As Kallis (2015b) explains, degrowth can liberate "conceptual space" for countries to identify their own ideas of well-being and "can provide space for the flourishing of alternative cosmovisions and practices in the South, such as *buen vivir* in Latin America or *ubuntu* in Africa." Thus, degrowth could help promote alternatives to Western development, which in many cases produces poverty, and these alternatives could guide pathways for increased social well-being.

Degrowth: a useful term for a social movement?

When learning about degrowth many students remark that the term "degrowth" is not very appealing, as the negativity of the word suggests having less and personal sacrifice. They explain that degrowth conjures images of life without technology and conveniences and that this is a very "un-American" notion that is unlikely to become popular. Through their research, Drews and Antal (2016) find that the word degrowth does have a downward orientation that fosters negative feelings, including fears of having less or forced austerity. They also find that the term in many cases "backfires" because it misleadingly suggests economic contraction and fosters the misinterpretation of degrowth as recession.

However, many scholars continue to support the use of the term "degrowth." The negative word or "missile word" was chosen intentionally to illustrate that it is confronting and challenging the hegemony of growth (Kallis 2015b). As argued by Kallis (2019: 273):

> Capitalism and its institutions are legitimated and reproduced in the name of growth. The imaginary and pursuit of growth survived even communist states' attack on capitalist relations. Unless we start changing the words we use and the images that come with them, we will remain stuck in the capitalist imaginary of growth.

In addition to explicitly being against growth, the term "degrowth" is much less likely to be coopted than more positive terms (Kallis 2018). Many approaches to address social and environmental problems have been coopted by the profit motive, undermining their effectiveness. Degrowth discourages cooptation because it represents a direct attack of growth and many scholars and activists continue to support the use of the term for this reason.

Others suggest using a more positive term that focuses on the benefits of degrowth. Schor (2010) uses the term "plenitude" to positively label living with enough rather than more and more. Others use the term "sufficiency" to stress, in a positive way, that all people will have enough to live (Parrique et al. 2019). Additional alternatives include: "beyond growth," "post-growth," "a-growth," "prosperity without growth," and "steady-state economy" (see Drews and Antal 2016). One approach is to highlight the ways that degrowth addresses personal dissatisfaction associated with work and free time as well as the misguided priorities guiding our society. For example, slogans such as "work less, waste less" or "well-being before profit" could highlight these points and paint degrowth as a way to increase personal fulfillment. These and other terms can emphasize how degrowth offers a simpler and "better" life with "more" desirable things like free-time and personal connection (Drews and Antal 2016).

The term degrowth may not be the most appealing term for building a social movement, but it does reinforce a rejection of hegemonic growth and is unlikely to be coopted for other uses. It is likely that different terms and framings could be more successful at garnering support in different contexts. Those already familiar with the negative impacts of the growth imperative are less likely to be turned away by the anti-growth emphasis. However, others might be more attracted to positive framings focused on the possible benefits of degrowth. It may be more beneficial overall to focus attention on the specific priorities, policies, and goals of degrowth rather than getting bogged down with the terminology. For example, abandoning GDP as an indicator of progress, implementing work time reduction, and increasing sharing and common resources can all be pursued and framed individually as positive changes for society. However, we also agree that "missile words" like degrowth are important to help undermine the dominance and pervasiveness of pro-growth ideology.

A rejection of unfeasibility and defeatism

We conclude by addressing a final critique of degrowth that pundits and students alike raise: a degrowth transition is not feasible and will never happen. The common rejection of degrowth because it is deemed unfeasible indicates just how much it contrasts with the priorities and configurations of our current social order. As Kallis and March (2015: 362) explain, degrowth "is a call for an altogether new, qualitatively different world that will evolve through confrontation with the existing one." Degrowth only seems unfeasible because the characteristics of the current social order appear to stand in the way. However, Marcuse (1967: 3) explains that:

> unfeasibility shows itself only after the fact. And it is not surprising that a project for social transformation is designated unfeasible because it has shown itself unrealized in history. . . the criterion of unfeasibility in this sense is inadequate because it may very well be the case that the realization of a revolutionary project is hindered by counterforces and countertendencies that can be and are overcome . . .

Marcuse (1967) further argues that we already have all the intellectual and material forces we need for positive social transformation and

> [t]hat they are not used for that purpose is to be attributed to the total mobilization of existing society against its own potential for liberation. But this situation in no way makes the idea of radical transformation itself a utopia.

We agree that degrowth represents a concrete utopia (Kallis 2018), a vision that is indeed possible with components already emerging in embryonic form. Yet its full realization remains constrained by the dominant assumptions that deem it unfeasible and support the ideology of growth. While a transition to degrowth may be desirable and possible, there are indeed significant challenges and barriers. Yet, this is no reason to succumb to defeatism. Only by continuing to confront the rationalities of growth can we work towards social changes to better support equality, well-being, and ecological flourishing. In other words, while there are certainly many obstacles to a degrowth transition, it is still worth pursuing. As Marcuse (1967: 6) explains: "An opposition is required that is free of all illusion but also of all defeatism, for through its mere existence defeatism betrays the possibility of freedom to the status quo."

6 Pathways for change

As protecting economic growth still takes precedent in global policy, the calls of scientists to change our system continue to be largely ignored. As described in Chapter 1, these scientists agree that if we do not radically change our social and economic systems we could reach critical thresholds resulting in social-ecological collapse. Some people and corporations are already planning to use the crisis to increase profits. While crisis and collapse could result in economic gain for a few, for most people—especially the least responsible and most vulnerable people in the global majority—the outlook is far from good. From a position of concern about ecosystems, biodiversity, and current and future generations of humans, we have examined degrowth as an alternative to the status quo that is possible and holds potential to justly alleviate the drivers of our environmental crisis.

While extensive thought has been devoted to what a degrowth transition might look like, less work has focused on the question of how a degrowth transition might occur. As explained by Gorz (1967), we can easily focus on the question of what to do when we are in power; however, the more immediate and challenging question is how "to create the means and will to get there." While few degrowth scholars have mapped out pathways for transformation (one exception discussed below), Gorz (1967), Wright (2010, 2019), and others have extensively theorized pathways for positive social transformation, and we apply these visions of transition here.

First, we summarize the work of D'Alisa and Kallis (2020), applying Gramscian theory to a degrowth transition. While in some cases a tension has emerged between calls for a bottom-up, grass-roots degrowth transition versus a top-down policy transition, many scholars agree that both are critical. Gramscian theory emphasizes the role of both civil and political society as essential for social change. Civil society is the arena where ideas, like the economic growth imperative, become widespread, and common sense or hegemonic. Political society is the arena of policy, law, enforcement, and the legitimation of power. D'Alisa and Kallis (2020) explain that from a Gramscian perspective change focused on civil or political society alone will be insufficient as political change requires the support of civil society (people are willing to accept changes in values and priorities), and changes in civil society at the grass-roots level will remain stymied and constrained by political institutions. Because the ideology of growth is reproduced in both civic and political spheres, a degrowth transition requires organizing in both:

> Transformation then involves a coevolutionary change between civil and political society. A degrowth transformation requires first social relationships and activities that provide viable livelihoods and produce in the ground, and not in the abstract, common senses that prioritize 'degrowth-oriented' values and objectives. In parallel, those who believe and live by these values have to organize politically for the implementation of policies that reflect these common senses.
>
> (D'Alisa and Kallis 2020: 7)

In line with this idea of an interrelated dual approach to social change, we apply the idea of "erosion" in Wright (2019) to discuss the necessary transformations in both ideology and in the social system to open up spaces for degrowth alternatives. Eroding includes both bottom-up and top-down strategies in the process of transcending capitalism, very much in line with Gramscian theory (D'Alisa and Kallis 2020).

Rather than an abrupt replacement of the current system, the notion of eroding suggests the system, and the ideologies that support it, can be weakened over time while alternatives are increased and become the new norm. While there is certainly no time to waste, we agree with Wright (2010, 2019) that a rapid social transition through violent means is not likely or desirable. In most cases, the outcomes of violent revolution have not been socially beneficial or sustainable (Wright 2010). Instead we describe the possibilities for a steady and meaningful transition through eroding away ideological and systemic obstacles and increasing the ideas, priorities, relationships, policies, and institutions that could support degrowth pathways. We want to emphasize that we are under no illusion that the processes described here would be easy or are likely to occur. We have detailed social and political barriers elsewhere, including a global right-wing shift, the lack of a coherent anti-capitalist social movement, and the likelihood of the continuing cooptation of degrowth-esque ideas (Stuart et al. 2020). Despite powerful opposition and the everyday reproduction of the status quo, the pathways described are still possible and worth pursuing.

The erosion of growth ideology

Ideology usually refers to our underlying beliefs and worldviews that shape how we understand the world and interpret new information and ideas. However, ideology has also been used to describe ideas that are specifically used to conceal the truth. As we and others have discussed elsewhere (Gunderson et al. 2018a; Hickel and Kallis 2019; Schor and Jorgenson 2019), "green growth" as a solution to our environmental crisis is an example of ideology. Green growth, like other ideologies, not only hides the truth but prevents the kind of changes necessary. Ideology is used to protect those who benefit the most from the maintenance of the current system. The challenge is to be able to identify ideology, refute it, and then shift the balance of power through building political support and social movements to demand change.

Indeed, people are unlikely to support political measures imposed upon them that they do not understand as necessary or beneficial. While "growth is good" is still the dominant paradigm, this notion is increasingly challenged and publicly debated. In addition to the scientists quoted in Chapter 1, activists are increasingly demanding that governments put "people before profit" and Greta Thurnberg specifically called out the "fairytales of eternal economic growth" in her speech at the United Nations. Even more mainstream economists, like Joseph Stiglitz, are calling for the end of GDP as the primary indicator of progress. There is growing agreement that GDP growth is not a legitimate measure of well-being and is leading us further into multiple crises (Stiglitz 2019a, 2019b). In summary, the sacred status of pro-growth ideology is being increasingly questioned and refuted in civil society and this is likely to increase in the near future.

As we illustrated in Chapter 5, economic growth is an inherent structural feature of, and a fundamental goal of, modern capitalism and the engine driving us further into environmental crisis. Increasingly this linkage is being made and exposed in books (e.g., Foster et al. 2011; Klein 2015; Wright and Nyberg 2015) and independent left-wing news and media outlets (e.g., *Common Dreams*, *Monthly Review*, and *Truthout*), although not widely in the mainstream media, excluding *The Guardian*. Despite increasing awareness of this connection, market-friendly solutions, and techno-fixes (see Chapter 2) illustrate how capitalism continues to attempt to resolve issues in its own way.

Yet, as the ineffectiveness of these solutions becomes more obvious, we are likely to see more environmental and social justice groups taking aim at capitalism and the growth paradigm.

As the flaws of pro-growth ideology are increasingly exposed, support is increasing for alternatives. Some of those who cast off the ideology of growth may choose to "escape" the system through creating new forms of work and living in the cracks of the current system (Wright 2019). New lifestyle trends, even in the highly consumptive US, indicate that more people at least have a desire to create a different world, though focusing on individual changes. Examples include voluntary minimalism or simplicity. In addition, buying used clothes and other items at thrift stores, garage sales, and flea markets is common. Another trend is "fix-it" clinics, offering ways to repair rather than replace goods, and more people are participating in community gardens and self-provisioning. These trends indicate an increased desire to move away from high consumptive lifestyles. Going even further, there are intentional communities and "nowtopias" prioritizing low-consumption, sharing, and relationship building (Demaria et al. 2019). In addition to these forms of "escape," many people also wish to directly challenge or resist the dominant system.

Wright (2019) explains that "resisting" largely refers to the work of social movements who oppose the state from the outside, aiming to influence the state through protesting and trouble-making. This form of resistance matches with Polanyi's description of the "double movement," Gorz's (1967) idea of "counter-powers," and Reich's (2016) call for "countervailing powers" for social transformation. Increasing forms of resistance, such as non-violent direct action, is critical to pressure governments to take-action and to further increase awareness among the public that the status quo is no longer acceptable. Such resistance is growing as seen through the actions of activist groups including, Fridays for Future, Extinction Rebellion, and the Sunrise Movement—increasing awareness and applying pressure on the state to rethink the prioritization of economic growth before people and the environment. While the scale of the climate movement is unprecedented, more, and sustained action is necessary.

Wright (2019: 119, 121) states that "the most vexing problem" and "the biggest puzzle" for emancipatory transformation is the creation of collective agency. The question remains: "who is going to participate in such struggles? Where is the collective agent capable of sustaining struggles to erode capitalism?" (Wright 2019: 117). Wright (2019) argued that most people are motivated by moral concerns rather than class or economic concerns. When youth activists demand that world leaders protect their future, they draw attention to the immorality of continuing with business as usual. Climate change is becoming a moral concern due to the obvious generational injustice: continued inaction on climate change knowingly leaves children exposed to a catastrophic future. This moral framing is also changing the political and legal terrain. For example, in 2019 the Dutch supreme court ruled that the government must act to protect its citizens from climate change. As figures like Greta Thunberg continue to emphasize the immorality of inaction, environmental movements are likely to grow.

The erosion of the growth system

In 2018, as a precursor to the United Nations Global Sustainable Development Report, a group of scientists released a report calling for a radical state-led global economic transition to address our environmental crisis (Järvensivu et al. 2019). They called for a new economic system, where "[i]ndividuals, organizations, and nations would approach the economy as a tool to enable a good life rather than as an end in itself." This system would "focus on life-improving and emissions-reducing goals rather than abstract economic goals." This again echoes the call to subordinate economic goals to social and ecological well-being, something that our current system, focused on prioritizing profit and economic growth, remains incapable of doing.

As discussed in the previous chapter, because we believe a defining characteristic of modern capitalism is perpetual growth and growth dependency, we believe that challenging growth also requires challenging capitalism. As stated before, this does not mean the abolition of all markets, but the abandonment of the growth imperative and all that comes with it: the normalization of prioritizing economic growth, using increases in productivity for more production rather than more leisure, etc. Because private ownership of the means of production is the major driver of the growth imperative, a livable future depends on our willingness to experiment with old and new forms of collective ownership and governance while building deeply democratic institutions to consciously avoid the social and ecological disasters of many twentieth century "socialist" projects. Industries that can be cooperatized (i.e., made into worker cooperatives) should be. Nationalization with a high degree of public governance may be the only possible model of collective ownership for large and complex industries that are harming the environment and humans for profits, such as the fossil fuel industry. Sectors that remain in private hands would require more stringent regulations. While less likely a decade ago, as of 2020, challenging capitalism is increasingly possible as political candidates self-identifying as democratic socialists gain support. These trends signify ripening conditions for system change.

For the system to radically change, it must be widely deemed inadequate. Schweickart (2016) posits that deep social change requires a legitimation crisis. Similarly, Gorz (1967: 4) argued that openings for social change can occur when it becomes clear that peoples' needs are not being met. As of 2020, environmental activists are drawing more and more attention to the failure of governments to protect future generation. Youth activists claim that governments are not doing their job and are not meeting their needs for a livable future (Carrington 2019). As stated by an activist in the Sunrise Movement: "If our leaders aren't willing to really address the crisis that we're facing right now, then they need to be replaced" (Horton et al. 2019). Social movements are not only necessary to challenge ideology, but to pressure the state into action. While these arguments are further politicized and expose the failures of the current system, the challenge remains connecting these sentiments to the transformations necessary.

Wright (2019) describes several ways that transformation can occur through the state. "Taming" involves reducing the harms of capitalism or treating the symptoms rather than replacing the system. However, taming strategies become increasingly insufficient as more evidence suggests that programs and policies that prioritize economic growth will fail to quickly and effectively address our environmental crisis (Hickel and Kallis 2019; Petersen et al. 2019; Schor and Jorgenson 2019). For example, new markets and technological innovations in line with capitalist goals have not resulted in emissions reductions that would keep warming within 1.5°C (Gunderson et al. 2018a, 2018b, 2018c; Stuart et al. 2019). If we listen to the scientists, we are far past the time for compromised approaches. Therefore, we need more meaningful policies that aim to protect people and the environment rather than appease those seeking profit.

Wright (2019) also describes strategies for "dismantling" through the state. Dismantling refers to state-directed incremental reforms such as the socialization of health care, education, transportation, and energy. In terms of policies for dismantling the drivers of our environmental crisis, we believe the most beneficial outcome would be the implementation of "non-reformist reforms" (Gorz 1967). As described by Kallis (2018: 136), these are

> reforms that, if they were to be implemented, would require the very contours of the system to change radically to accommodate

them. And reforms that, simple and commonsensical as they are, expose the irrationality of the system that makes them seem impossible.

Gorz (1967) explained that these reforms can advance a radical transformation of society and act as part of a "transitional program" (Löwy 2015: 37). In other words, these reforms change the terrain of what is possible and open up opportunities for more radical system change.

What might these "non-reformist reforms" look like? First, a critical first step would be, not only transitioning to renewable energy as soon as possible, but also keeping remaining fossil fuels in the ground through fossil fuel nationalization (e.g., see Gowan 2018; Skandier 2018). In addition, many of the changes we described in Chapter 4 would represent meaningful non-reformist reforms. Socializing energy systems through community energy initiatives can help foster a transition to renewables and reducing total energy use (e.g., Kunze and Becker 2015; Gunderson et al. 2018b). Economic democracy, for example, worker-owned cooperatives and public banks, can open up spaces for communities to address climate change (e.g., Boillat et al. 2012; Johanisova and Wolf 2012). In addition, work time reduction can significantly reduce GHG emissions through reducing overall resource and energy use (e.g., Rosnick and Weisbrot 2006; Knight et al. 2013; Rosnick 2013; Fitzgerald et al. 2015; Schor 2015). Lastly, restrictions on advertising and policies to reduce resource use and consumption are critical to reducing carbon emissions (Cosme et al. 2017; Hickel 2019c). Any one of these reforms alone would likely alter conditions in ways that would open the door for further change. While a piece-meal approach is possible, so is a comprehensive vision and plan for many related reforms.

In 2018, the Green New Deal (GND, House Resolution 109) was introduced in the US Congress. Could the GND represent a suite of "non-reformist reforms"? The GND is currently a list of goals, without the details of the policies that would achieve these goals. Here we outline what might help a GND to most effectively and justly address our environmental crisis:

- While the GND includes the target of achieving net-zero emissions by 2050 and a transition to renewable energy, it does not directly call for curtailing or ending fossil fuel use—a necessary step.
- In line with degrowth, the GND supports community-based energy and climate-focused initiatives including building "wealth and

community ownership" and "investments for community-defined projects and strategies," but an additional focus on (re)commoning energy is missing.

• The promotion of economic democracy is clear: the GND promotes public banks and worker-cooperatives. It also affirms workers' rights and proposes a job guarantee. However, the GND does not mention work-time reduction or job sharing that could help achieve social and environmental goals.

• Also absent in the GND is an intention to limit advertising and consumption. Instead we see a call for "growth in clean manufacturing" and to "invest in infrastructure and industry" both goals in accord with popular pro-growth rhetoric. This language indicates that further work is needed to counter the ideology of growth and build political support for degrowth pathways.

While the GND does not yet resemble the "non-reformist reforms" necessary for a degrowth transition, it could represent a step in that direction. It does not directly challenge economic growth, yet it does indicate that there is a growing desire to address our environmental crisis along with widening economic inequality. Uniting those concerned with environmental and economic injustices creates a stronger force to confront the current system. However, the challenge remains linking these concerns to an awareness of the underlying driver of this crisis: the economic growth imperative. While the future is impossible to predict, as scientists, economists, scholars, activists, and others repeatedly call attention to the malignant effects of economic growth, pro-growth ideology and the system perpetuating this ideology are likely to continue to erode. Given what is at stake, the speed of this erosion is critical.

Toward a social tipping point

Despite significant obstacles and challenges, calls for changing our current system are getting louder and could result in a social tipping point. In 2020, Otto et al. published an article titled, "Social tipping dynamics for stabilizing Earth's climate by 2050" in the *Proceedings of the National Academy of Sciences*. They examine how social tipping points might open pathways for addressing the climate crisis. They define a social tipping point as a small change that triggers larger-scale changes and "that inevitably and often irreversibly lead to a qualitatively different state of the social system" (Otto et al. 2020: 2355). While revolutionary changes may occur quickly in response to environmental catastrophes, Ott et al. (2020) explain that social tipping points can also lead to social transformation through purposeful interventions. The latter has a much greater potential for socially just and ecologically beneficial outcomes.

While we cannot predict if and when a social tipping point will occur, certain signs indicate that conditions may be ripening for change. Throughout history, moral standards shift and what was once deemed socially acceptable can change quickly along with associated norms, rules, and policies. In agreement with Wright (2019), Otto et al. (2020: 2361) state that moral concerns can be critical for reaching social tipping points and predict "increased recognition of the intergenerationally unethical and immoral character of fossil fuels that will furthermore strengthen the legitimacy of carbon mitigation policies." They argue the climate movement is already causing significant shifts in worldviews, norms, and values—changing the terrain of what is possible. While this all may be true, there are still significant obstacles due to the strength of forces protecting the status quo.

Given the scientific projections and the environmental impacts already occurring, an increasing number of people are finding that maintaining the status quo is immoral. While often painted as simply a political issue, the environmental crisis is very much a moral issue, a human issue, and an issue about life itself. It was made political because those with great power have chosen to resist the changes necessary through political means. As a result, many people might think that the content of this book is highly controversial. Yet, if this book examines possible pathways to best protect ecosystems, species, and current and future generations of humans, is that truly controversial? Is it not our moral imperative as a thoughtful species to consider how to achieve a just and sustainable future?

Social tipping points may be reached due to unexpected events. We are writing this book in the spring of 2020 during the Covid-19 pandemic. The pandemic has further exposed the flaws of the capitalist system and revealed mass social vulnerability. Policies in line with a degrowth transition are being increasingly discussed as the pandemic shifts the political dialogue. For example, even the editorial board of the moderate London-based newspaper *The Financial Times* proposed "radical reforms" in a piece published on April 4:

> Radical reforms—reversing the prevailing policy direction of the last four decades—will need to be put on the table . . . Policies until recently considered eccentric, such as basic income and wealth taxes, will have to be in the mix.

In a newspaper publication, 170 Dutch academics called for a radical economic transition in response to Covid-19 and specifically to implement the following strategies (Feola 2020):

1   a move away from "development" focused on aggregate GDP growth;
2   an economic framework focused on redistribution;
3   transformation towards regenerative agriculture;
4   reduction of consumption and travel;
5   debt cancellation.

As precarity increases globally, strategies in-line with degrowth are making more and more sense.

In addition, the Covid-19 pandemic is providing an opportunity to see how individuals and institutions could adapt to a degrowth transition. To be clear, degrowth would be a planned economic contraction with social safety nets in place, as opposed to the current response in the US: a tremendously harmful recession with, despite the chaos, new neoliberal pseudo-stimulus packages to redistribute wealth upwards. However, the Covid-19 pandemic illustrates that it is possible for societies to quickly shift to lower-carbon lifestyles: working less, consuming less, and traveling less. It also reveals how policies like work sharing (e.g., Germany's response), wealth taxes, and basic income—or a similar program such as governments subsidizing salaries for workers to stay home (e.g., Denmark's response)—could support a transition. The pandemic also further illustrates the many flaws of a system prioritizing economic growth, reinforcing the need for system change and a more just, post-growth alternative.

Moving beyond debating *if* the current system should change, we should be debating specifically *how* we should change our social and economic system. In this book, we have examined degrowth as a possible path forward to effectively and justly address our environmental crisis. As more people acknowledge that change is necessary, degrowth may become more widely discussed and considered. As this happens, the relationships between capitalism, economic growth, and our environmental crisis need to be made clear. Moving forward, we recommend increasing opportunities for deeply democratic and deliberative processes where groups of citizens can learn about, discuss, and debate the possible options for a new system. Examples such as participatory budgeting and citizens assemblies provide models of how people can make informed choices about their own future. The degrowth ideas presented here, along with many others, could be made accessible and available as options.

As climate change and biodiversity loss accelerate, we go deeper into a state of crisis: a state where the current system can no longer be maintained. The environmental crisis is becoming more severe and will affect human lives more obviously each year. As these impacts are experienced unequally, and as some benefit while many more suffer, the immorality of the situation will become ever clearer. When we finally reach a social tipping point, we will be in a much stronger position to make choices if we have already identified what should be prioritized, examined the alternatives, collaborated democratically to set goals, and evaluated pathways for positive social change. Ideas from degrowth could be included in this process and help us to define the parameters for a new set of social, ecological, and economic relations.

References

Alcott, B. 2005. Jevons' paradox. *Ecological Economics*, 54(1): 9–21.

Alexander, S., and Yacoumis, P. 2018. Degrowth, energy descent, and 'low-tech' living: Potential pathways for increased resilience in times of crisis. *Journal of Cleaner Production*, 197: 1840–1848.

Anderson, K. 2015. Talks in the city of light generate more heat. *Nature News*, 528(7583): 437.

Anderson, K., and Bows, A. 2011. Beyond 'dangerous' climate change: Emission scenarios for a new world. *Philosophical Transactions of the Royal Society A: Mathematical, Physical and Engineering Sciences*, 369(1934): 20–44.

Anderson, K., and Peters, G. 2016. The trouble with negative emissions. *Science*, 354(6309): 182–183.

Archer, R. 1995. *Economic Democracy: The Politics of Feasible Socialism*. Oxford: Clarendon Press.

Baer, H. 2019. Toward democratic eco-socialism as the next world system. The Next System Project. https://thenextsystem.org/toward-democratic-eco-socialism-as-the-next-world-system.

Baik, E., Sanchez, D.L., Turner, P.A., Mach, K.J., Field, C.B., and Benson, S.M. 2018. Geospatial analysis of near-term potential for carbon-negative bioenergy in the United States. *Proceedings of the National Academy of Sciences*, 115(13): 3290–3295.

Barca, S. 2019. The labor(s) of degrowth. *Capitalism Nature Socialism*, 30(2): 207–216.

Barnosky, A.D., Matzke, N., Tomiya, S., Wogan, G.O., Swartz, B., Quental, T.B., ... Mersey, B. 2011. Has the earth's sixth mass extinction already arrived? *Nature*, 471(7336): 51.

Bayon, D. 2015. Unions. In *Degrowth: A Vocabulary for a New Era*, edited by G. D'Alisa, F. Demaria, and G. Kallis, 181–191. New York: Routledge.

Bithas, K., and Kalimeris, P. 2018. Unmasking decoupling: Redefining the resource intensity of the Economy. *Science of the Total Environment*, 619–620: 338–351.

Bloemmen, M., Bobulescu, R., Le, N.T., and Vitari, C. 2015. Microeconomic degrowth: The case of community supported agriculture. *Ecological Economics*, 112: 110–115.

Bodhi, N., Brook, B., and Bradshaw, C. 2009. Causes and consequences of species extinctions. *The Princeton Guide to Ecology*, 1: 514–520.

Boillat, S., Gerber, J.F., and Funes-Monzote, F.R. 2012. What economic democracy for degrowth? Some comments on the contribution of socialist models and Cuban agroecology. *Futures*, 44(6): 600–607.

Bollier, D. 2014. *Think Like a Commoner: A Short Introduction to the Life of the Commons*. Gabriola Island: New Society.

Boucher, O., Randall, D., Artaxo, P., Bretherton, C., Feingold, G., Forster, P., ... Zhang, X.Y. 2013. Clouds and aerosols. In *Climate Change 2013: The Physical Science Basis*, edited by T.F. Stocker, D. Qin, G.K. Plattner, M. Tignor, S.K. Allen, J. Boschung, ... P.M. Midgley. Cambridge and New York: Cambridge University Press.

Brockington, D., and Duffy, R. 2010. Capitalism and conservation: The production and reproduction of biodiversity conservation. *Antipode*, 42(3): 469–484.

Brossmann, J., and Islar, M. 2019. Living degrowth? Investigating degrowth practices through performative methods. *Sustainability Science*, 15: 917–930.

Brulle, R.J., and Dunlap, R.E. 2015. Sociology and global climate change. In *Climate Change and Society: Sociological Perspectives*, edited by R.E. Dunlap, and R.J. Brulle, 1–31. New York: Oxford University Press.

Buch-Hansen, H., and Koch, M. 2019. Degrowth through income and wealth caps? *Ecological Economics*, 160: 264–271.

Bull, J.W., Suttle, K.B., Gordon, A., Singh, N.J., and Milner-Gulland, E.J. 2013. Biodiversity offsets in theory and practice. *Oryx*, 47(3): 369–380.

Bulman, M. 2018. German workers win right to 28-hour week following industrial action. Independent. February 11, 2018. https://www.independent.co.uk/news/world/europe/german-workers-right-28hour-week-trade-union-industrial-action-ig-metall-a8205751.html.

Burke, P.J., Shahiduzzaman, M., and Stern, D.I. 2015. Carbon dioxide emissions in the short run: The rate and sources of economic growth matter. *Global Environmental Change-Human and Policy Dimensions*, 33: 109–121.

Büscher, B., Sullivan, S., Neves, K., Igoe, J., and Brockington, D. 2012. Towards a synthesized critique of neoliberal biodiversity conservation. *Capitalism Nature Socialism*, 23(2): 4–30.

Byrne, J., Martinez, C., and Ruggero, C. 2009. Relocating energy in the social commons: Ideas for a sustainable energy utility. *Bulletin of Science, Technology & Society*, 29(2): 81–94.

Carrington, D. 2019. Youth climate strikers: 'We are going to change the fate of humanity'. *The Guardian*. March 1, 2019.

Catlin, J.R., and Wang, Y.T. 2013. Recycling gone bad: When the option to recycle increases resource consumption. *Journal of Consumer Psychology*, 23: 122–127.

Cavlovic, T.A., Baker, K.H., Berrens, R.P., and Gawande, K. 2000. A meta-analysis of environmental Kuznets curve studies. *Agricultural and Resource Economics Review*, 29: 32–42.

CBS News. 2019. Most Americans say climate change should be addressed now—CBS news poll. https://www.cbsnews.com/news/cbs-news-poll-most-americans-say-climate-change-should-be-addressed-now-2019-09-15/.

Ceballos, G., Ehrlich, P.R., Barnosky, A.D., García, A., Pringle, R.M., and Palmer, T.M. 2015. Accelerated modern human–induced species losses: Entering the sixth mass extinction. *Science Advances*, 1(5): 1400253.

Ceballos, G., Ehrlich, P.R., and Dirzo, R. 2017. Biological annihilation via the ongoing sixth mass extinction signaled by vertebrate population losses and declines. *Proceedings of the National Academy of Sciences*, 114(30): E6089–E6096.

Chancel, L., and Piketty, T. 2015. Carbon and inequality: From Kyoto to Paris. *Paris School of Economics*. Accessed August 10, 2020. https://halshs.archives-ouvertes.fr/halshs-02655266/document.

Circle Economy. 2020. https://www.circularity-gap.world/2020.

Clark, B., and Foster, J.B. 2001. William Stanley Jevons and The Coal Question – An introduction to Jevons's "Of the economy of fuel". *Organization & Environment*, 14(1): 93–98.

Clark, B., Foster, J., and York, R. 2010. *The Ecological Rift: Capitalism's War on the Earth*. New York: Monthly Review Press.

Clement, M.T. 2011. The Jevons paradox and anthropogenic global warming: A panel analysis of state-level carbon emissions in the United States, 1963–1997. *Society & Natural Resources*, 24(9): 951–961.

Climate Action Tracker. 2019. USA: Country summary. https://climateactiontracker.org/countries/usa/.

Conley, J. 2019. Tipping point: UN biodiversity chief warns burning of Amazon could lead to 'Cascading collapse of natural systems'. *Common Dreams*, August 30, 2019.

Corporate Europe Observatory. 2015. EU emissions trading: 5 reasons to scrap the ETS. https://corporateurope.org/environment/2015/10/eu-emissions-trading-5-reasons-scrap-ets.

Cosme, I., Santos, R., and O'Neill, D.W. 2017. Assessing the degrowth discourse: A review and analysis of academic degrowth policy proposals. *Journal of Cleaner Production*, 149: 321–334.

Czech, B., Mills Busa, J.H., and Brown, R.M. 2012. Effects of economic growth on biodiversity in the United States. *Natural Resources Forum*, 36(3): 160–166.

D'Alisa, G., and Kallis, G. 2020. Degrowth and the state. *Ecological Economics*, 169(C). Accessed August 10, 2020. https://doi.org/10.1016/j.ecolecon.2019.106486.

D'Allessandro, S., Dittmer, K., Distefano, T., and Cieplinski, A. 2018. EUROGREEN model of job creation in a post-growth economy. The Greens and EFA in the European Parliament.

Daly, H. 2013. A further critique of growth economics. *Ecological Economics*, 88: 20–24.

Debord, G. 1983. *Society of the Spectacle*. Detroit: Black and Red.

Dechezleprêtre, A., Nachtigall, D., and Venmans, F. 2018. The joint impact of the European Union emissions trading system on carbon emissions and economic performance. OECD Economics Department Working Papers, No. 1515. Paris: OECD Publishing.

Demaria, F., Kallis, G., and Bakker, K. 2019. Geographies of degrowth: Nowtopias, resurgences and the decolonization of imaginaries and places. *Environment and Planning E: Nature and Space*, 2(3): 431–450.

Dengler, C., and Seebacher, L.M. 2019. What about the global south? Towards a feminist decolonial degrowth approach. *Ecological Economics*, 157: 246–252.

Dickman, A., and Skinner, G. 2019. Ipsos MORI. Retrieved from https://www.ipsos.com/ipsos-mori/en-uk/concern-about-climate-change-reaches-record-levels-half-now-very-concerned.

Dietz, T. 2015. Prolegomenon to a structural human ecology of human well-being. *Sociology of Development*, 1(1): 123–148.

Dietz, T., Gardner, G.T., Gilligan, J., Stern, P.C., and Vandenbergh, M.P. 2009. Household actions can provide a behavioral wedge to rapidly reduce US carbon emissions. *Proceedings of the National Academy of Sciences of the United States of America*, 106(44): 18452–18456.

Dietz, T., Rosa, E.A., and York, R. 2012. Environmentally efficient well-being: Is there a Kuznets curve? *Applied Geography*, 32(1): 21–28.

Drews, S., and Antal, M. 2016. Degrowth: A "missile word" that backfires? *Ecological Economics*, 126: 182–187.

Duffy, R. 2008. Neoliberalising nature: Global networks and ecotourism development in Madagasgar. *Journal of Sustainable Tourism*, 16(3): 327–344.

Earp, H.N.S., and Romeiro, A.R. 2015. The entropy law and the impossibility of perpetual economic growth. *Open Journal of Applied Sciences*, 5(10): 641–650.

Easterlin, R.A., Mcvey, L.A., Switek, M., Sawangfa, O., and Zweig, J.S. 2010. The happiness-income paradox revisited. *Proceedings of the National Academy of Sciences of the United States of America*, 107(52): 22463–22468.

Economist Intelligence Unit. 2019. *Democracy Index 2018: Me Too? Political Participation, Protest and Democracy.* London: Economist Intelligence Unit.

EOD (Earth Overshoot Day). 2019. https://www.overshootday.org/.

Feng, K., Davis, S.J., Sun, L., and Hubacek, K. 2015. Drivers of the US CO 2 emissions 1997–2013. *Nature Communications*, 6: 7714.

Feola, G. 2020. Manifesto for post-neoliberal development: Five policy strategies for the Netherlands after the Covid-19 crisis. Ontgroei. https://ontgroei.degrowth.net/manifesto-for-post-neoliberal-development-five-policy-strategies-for-the-netherlands-after-the-covid-19-crisis/.

Ferraro, A.J., Highwood, E.J., and Charlton-Perez, A.J. 2014. Weakened tropical circulation and reduced precipitation in response to geoengineering. *Environmental Research Letters*, 9(1): 014001.

Fitzgerald, J.B., Jorgenson, A.K., and Clark, B. 2015. Energy consumption and working hours: A longitudinal study of developed and developing nations, 1990–2008. *Environmental Sociology*, 3(1): 213–223.

Foster, J.B. 2010. Why ecological revolution. *Monthly Review*, 61(8), https://monthlyreview.org/2010/01/01/why-ecological-revolution/

Foster, J.B., Clark, B., and York, R. 2009. The Midas effect: A critique of climate change economics. *Development and Change,* 40(6): 1085–1097.

Fridahl, M. 2017. Socio-political prioritization of bioenergy with carbon capture and storage. *Energy Policy*, 104: 89–99.

Fuss, S., Canadell, J.G., Peters, G.P., Tavoni, M., Andrew, R.M., Ciais, P., ... Yamagata, Y. 2014. Betting on negative emissions. *Nature Climate Change*, 4(10): 850–853.

Gabriel, C.A., and Bond, C. 2019. Need, entitlement and desert: A distributive justice framework for consumption degrowth. *Ecological Economics*, 156: 327–336.

Galbraith, K. 1958. *The Affluent Society*. Boston: Houghton Mifflin.

Geyer, R., and Rihani, S. 2012. *Complexity and Public Policy: A New Approach to 21st Century Politics, Policy and Society*. New York: Routledge.

Gills, B., and Morgan, J. 2019. Global climate emergency: After COP24, climate science, urgency, and the threat to humanity. *Globalizations*, 1–19. https://doi.org/10.1080/14747731.2019.1669915.

Global Financial Integrity. 2016. New report on unrecorded capital flight finds developing countries are net-creditors to the rest of the world. https://gfintegrity.org/press-release/new-report-on-unrecorded-capital-flight-finds-developing-countries-are-net-creditors-to-the-rest-of-the-world/. Accessed March 31, 2020.

Gómez-Baggethun, E. 2020. More is more: Scaling political ecology within limits to growth. *Political Geography*, 76: 102095.

Goodstein, E. 1999. *The Trade-Off Myth: Fact and Fiction about Jobs and the Environment*. Washington, DC: Island Press.

Gorz, A. 1967. *Strategy for Labor*. Boston, MA: Beacon Press.

Gowan, P. 2018. A plan to nationalize fossil-fuel companies. *Jacobin*. https://www.jacobinmag.com/2018/03/nationalize-fossil-fuel-companies-climate-change.

Granados, J.A.T., and Spash, C.L. 2019. Policies to reduce CO_2 emissions: Fallacies and evidence from the United States and California. *Environmental Science & Policy*, 94: 262–266.

Green, A., Carter, J., Williams, R., Dorling, D., Bendell, J., Gibson, I., ... Ali, S. 2018. Facts about our ecological crisis are incontrovertible: We must take action. *TheGuardian*.https://www.theguardian.com/environment/2018/oct/26/facts-about-our-ecological-crisis-are-incontrovertible-we-must-take-action.

Green New Deal. H.R. 109. 2019. https://www.congress.gov/bill/116th-congress/house-resolution/109.

Griner, D. 2017. 18 bullish stats about the State of U.S. advertising. Adweek. https://www.adweek.com/agencies/18-bullish-stats-about-the-state-of-u-s-advertising/.

Grubler, A., Wilson, C., Bento, N., Boza-Kiss, B., Krey, V., McCollum, D.L., ... Valin, H. 2018. A low energy demand scenario for meeting the 1.5°C target and sustainable development goals without negative emissions technologies. *Nature Energy*, 3(6): 515–527. https://doi.org/10.1038/s41560-018-0172-6.

Grunwald, A. 2018. Diverging pathways to overcoming the environmental crisis: A critique of eco-modernism from a technology assessment perspective. *Journal of Cleaner Production*, 197: 1854–1862.

Gunderson, R. 2018. Global environmental governance should be participatory: Five problems of scale. *International Sociology*, 33(6): 715–737.

Gunderson, R. 2019. Work time reduction and economic democracy as climate change mitigation strategies: Or why the climate needs a renewed labor movement. *Journal of Environmental Studies and Sciences*, 9(1): 35–44.

Gunderson, R., Stuart, D., and Petersen, B. 2018a. Ideological obstacles to effective climate policy: The greening of markets, technology, and growth. *Capital & Class*, 42(1): 133–160.

Gunderson, R., Stuart, D., and Petersen, B. 2018b. A critical examination of geoengineering: Economic and technological rationality in social context. *Sustainability*, 10(1): 269.

Gunderson, R., Stuart, D., Petersen, B., and Yun, S.J. 2018c. Social conditions to better realize the environmental gains of alternative energy: Degrowth and collective ownership. *Futures*, 99: 36–44.

Gunderson, R., Stuart, D., and Petersen, B. 2019. The political economy of geoengineering as plan B: Technological rationality, moral hazard, and new technology. *New Political Economy*, 24(5): 696–715.

Hall, C.A.S., Lambert, J.G., and Balogh, S.B. 2014. EROI of different fuels and the implications for society. *Energy Policy*, 64: 141–152. https://doi.org/10.1016/j.enpol.2013.05.049.

Hamilton, C. 2013. *Earthmasters: The Dawn of the Age of Climate Engineering.* Padstow: Yale University Press.

Hardin, G. 1968. The tragedy of the commons. *Science*, 162: 1243–1248.

Harper, A. 2017. Germany's biggest union is fighting for a 28 hour working week—here's how the UK could follow suit. *The Independent*, October 12. https://www.independent.co.uk/voices/four-day-working-week-german-union-28-hours-uk-fight-for-the-same-a7996261.html.

Harvey, D. 2014. *Seventeen Contradictions and the End of Capitalism.* New York: Oxford University Press.

Heikkurinen, P., Lozanoska, J., and Tosi, P. 2019. Activities of degrowth and political change. *Journal of Cleaner Production*, 211: 555–565.

Helfrich, S., and Bollier, D. 2015. Commons. In *Degrowth: A Vocabulary for a New Era*, edited by G. D'Alisa, F. Demaria, and G. Kallis, 75–78. New York: Routledge.

Hickel, J. 2017. *The Divide: A Brief Guide to Global Inequality and Its Solutions.* New York: Random House.

Hickel, J. 2019a. Degrowth: A theory of radical abundance. *Real-World Economic Review*, 87: 54–68.

Hickel, J. 2019b. The contradiction of the sustainable development goals: Growth versus ecology on a finite planet. *Sustainable Development*, 27(5): 873–884.

Hickel, J. 2019c. Is it possible to achieve a good life for all within planetary boundaries? *Third World Quarterly*, 40(1): 18–35.

Hickel, J., and Kallis, G. 2019. Is green growth possible? *New Political Economy*, 25(4): 469–486.

Hoffman, U. 2016. Can green growth really work? In *Green Growth: Ideology, Political Economy and the Alternatives*, edited by G. Dale, M. Mathai, and J. Oliviera. London: Zed Books.

Horkheimer, M., and Adorno, T.W. 1969. *Dialectic of Enlightenment*. New York: Continuum.

Horton, A., McClinton, D., and Aratani, L. 2019. Can they save us? Meet the climate kids fighting to fix the planet. *The Guardian*. March 4, 2019.

Igoe, J., and Brockington, D. 2007. Neoliberal conservation: A brief introduction. *Conservation and Society*, 5(4): 432–449.

Igoe, J., Neves, K., and Brockington, D. 2010. A spectacular eco-tour around the historic bloc: Theorising the convergence of biodiversity conservation and capitalist expansion. *Antipode*, 42(3): 486–512.

IPBES (Intergovernmental Science-Policy Platform on Biodiversity and Ecosystem Services). 2019a. Summary for policymakers of the global assessment report on biodiversity and ecosystem services of the Intergovernmental Science-Policy Platform on Biodiversity and Ecosystem Services. https://www.ipbes.net/global-assessment-report-biodiversity-ecosystem-services.

IPBES. 2019b. Media release. https://ipbes.net/news/Media-Release-Global-Assessment.

IPCC (Intergovernmental Panel on Climate Change). 2018. Summary for policymakers. In *Global Warming of 1.5°C*. Geneva, Switzerland: World Meteorological Organization. Accessed December 13, 2018. http://www.people-press.org/2015/01/15/.

Jackson, T. 2009. *Prosperity without Growth*. London: Earthscan.

Järvensivu, P., Toivanen, T., Vadén, T., Lähde, V., Majava, A., and Eronen, J.T. 2019. Governance of economic transition. *Global Sustainable Development Report*. Accessed August 10, 2020. https://researchportal.helsinki.fi/en/publications/governance-of-economic-transition-invited-background-document-for

Jarvis, H. 2019. Sharing, togetherness and intentional degrowth. *Progress in Human Geography*, 43(2): 256–275.

Jensen, D. 2009. Forget shorter showers. *Orion Magazine*. Accessed August 10, 2020. https://orionmagazine.org/article/forget-shorter-showers/.

Johanisova, N., and Wolf, S. 2012. Economic democracy: A path for the future? *Futures*, 44(6): 562–570.

Jorgenson, A.K., and Clark, B. 2012. Are the economy and the environment decoupling? A comparative international study, 1960–2005. *American Journal of Sociology*, 118(1): 1–44.

Kallis, G. 2015a. The left should embrace degrowth. https://newint.org/features/web-exclusive/2015/11/05/left-degrowth.

Kallis, G. 2015b. The degrowth alternative. Great Transition Initiative. https://greattransition.org/publication/the-degrowth-alternative.

Kallis, G. 2015c. Yes, we can propser without growth: 10 policy proposals for the new left. *Common Dreams*. https://www.commondreams.org/views/2015/01/28/yes-we-can-prosper-without-growth-10-policy-proposals-new-left

Kallis, G. 2017. Radical dematerialization and degrowth. *Philosophical Transactions of the Royal Society A: Mathematical, Physical and Engineering Sciences*, 375(2095): 20160383.

Kallis, G. 2018. *Degrowth*. Newcastle upon Tyne: Agenda Publishing.

Kallis, G. 2019. Capitalism, socialism, degrowth: A rejoinder. *Capitalism Nature Socialism*, 30(2): 267–273.

Kallis, G., Kerschner, C., and Martinez-Alier, J. 2012. The economics of degrowth. *Ecological Economics*, 84: 172–180.

Kallis, G., and March, H. 2015. Imaginaries of hope: The utopianism of degrowth. *Annals of the Association of American Geographers*, 105(2): 360–368.

Keith, D.W. 2013. *A Case for Climate Engineering*. Boston: MIT Press.

Khmara, Y., and Kronenberg, J. 2018. Degrowth in business: An oxymoron or a viable business model for sustainability? *Journal of Cleaner Production,* 177: 721–731.

Klein, N. 2014. *This Changes Everything: Capitalism vs. the Climate*. New York: Simon and Schuster.

Klein, N. 2015. *This Changes Everything: Capitalism vs. the Climate*. New York: Simon and Schuster.

Knight, K.W., Rosa, E.A., and Schor, J.B. 2013. Could working less reduce pressures on the environment? A cross-national panel analysis of OECD countries, 1970–2007. *Global Environmental Change-Human and Policy Dimensions*, 23(4): 691–700.

Knight, K., and Schor, J. 2014. Economic growth and climate change: A cross-national analysis of territorial and consumption-based carbon emissions in high-income countries. *Sustainability*, 6(6): 3722–3731.

Kunze, C., and Becker, S. 2015. Collective ownership in renewable energy and opportunities for sustainable degrowth. *Sustainability Science*, 10: 425–437.

LaJeunesse, R. 2009. *Worktime Regulation as Sustainable Full Employment Strategy: The Social Effort Bargain*. New York: Routledge.

Leiden University. 2018. Transition to renewable energy requires more space—but it will be much cleaner. Retrieved from https://www.universiteitleiden.nl/en/news/2018/08/publicatie-paul-behrens-sustainable-energy.

Lenton, T.M., Rockström, J., Gaffney, O., Rahmstorf, S., Richardson, K., Steffen, W., and Schellnhuber, H.J. 2019. Climate tipping points—too risky to bet against. Nature, 575: 592–595.

Lohmann, L. 2005. Marketing and making carbon dumps: Commodification, calculation and counterfactuals in climate change mitigation. *Science as Culture*, 14(3): 203–235.

Lohmann, L. 2010. Uncertainty markets and carbon markets: Variations on a Polanyian theme', *New Political Economy*, 15(2): 225–254.

Lovejoy, T.E. 2017. Extinction tsunami can be avoided. *Proceedings of the National Academy of Sciences of the United States of America*, 114(32): 8440–8441.

Löwy, M. 2006. Why ecosocialism: For a red-green future. Great Transition Initiative. https://greattransition.org/publication/why-ecosocialism-red-green-future.

Löwy, M. 2015. *Ecosocialism: A Radiacal Alternative to Capitalis Catastrophe.* Chicago, IL: Haymarket Books.

Malcom, J., Schwartz, M.W., Evansen, M., Ripple, W.J., Polasky, S., Gerber, L.R., Lovejoy, T.E., Talbot, L.M., Miller, J.R.B., and Signatories. 2019. Solve the biodiversity crisis with funding. *Science*, 365(6459): 1256–1256.

Marcuse, H. 1964. *One-Dimensional Man: The Ideology of Advanced Industrial Society.* Boston, MA: Beacon.

Marcuse, H. 1967. The end of Utopia. Lecture. https://www.marxists.org/reference/archive/marcuse/works/1967/end-utopia.htm.

Mardani, A., Streimikiene, D., Cavallaro, F., Loganathan, N., and Khoshnoudi, M. 2019. Carbon dioxide (CO2) emissions and economic growth: A systematic review of two decades of research from 1995 to 2017. *Science of the Total Environment*, 649: 31–49.

Marlon, J., Howe, P., Mildenberger, M., Leiserowitz, A., and Wang, X. 2019. Yale's website for climate opinion data. https://climatecommunication.yale.edu/visualizations-data/ycom-us/.

Martin, R., Muuls, M., and Wagner, U.J. 2016. The impact of the European Union emissions trading scheme on regulated firms: what is the evidence after ten years? *Review of Environmental Economics and Policy*, 10(1): 129–148.

Martinez-Alier, J. 1992. Ecological economics and concrete utopias. *Utopian Studies*, 3(1): 39–52.

Mazar, N., and Zhong, C.B. 2010. Do green products make us better people? *Psychological Science*, 21: 494–498.

Mercator Research Institute on Global Commons and Climate Change. 2017. The Mercator research institute. Accessed October 12, 2017. https://www.mcc-berlin.net/en/research.html.

Molotsky, I. 1988. Reagan Vetoes Bill putting limits on TV programming for children. *The New York Times.* November 7, 1988. https://www.nytimes.com/1988/11/07/us/reagan-vetoes-bill-putting-limits-on-tv-programming-for-children.html.

Muûls, M., Colmer, J., Martin, R., and Wagner, U. 2016. Evaluating the EU emissions trading system: Take it or leave it?: An assessment of the data after ten years'. *Grantham Institute Briefing Paper No. 21.* London: Imperial College.

National Academies of Sciences, Engineering, and Medicine. 2018. *Negative Emissions Technologies and Reliable Sequestration: A Research Agenda.* Washington, DC: The National Academies Press. https://doi.org/10.17226/25259.

Nicolas, B., Chèze, B., Alberola, E., and Chevallier, J. 2014. The CO_2 emissions of the European power sector: Economic drivers and the climate-energy policies' contribution. CDC Climate Research. Working Paper N 2014–17.

O'Connor, J. 1998. *Natural Causes: Essays in Ecological Marxism.* New York: Guilford Press.

O'Neill, D.W. 2012. Measuring progress in the degrowth transition to a steady state economy. *Ecological Economics*, 84: 221–231.

Ostrom, E. 1990. *Governing the Commons: The Evolution of Institutions for Collective Action.* Cambridge: Cambridge University Press.

Otero, I., Farrell, K.N., Pueyo, S., Kallis, G., Kehoe, L., Haberl, H., Plutzar, C., Hobson, P., García-Márquez, J., Rodríguez-Labajos, B. and Martin, J.L., 2020. Biodiversity policy beyond economic growth. *Conservation Letters*, p.e12713.

Otto, I.M., Donges, J.F., Cremades, R., Bhowmik, A., Hewitt, R.J., Lucht, W., ... Lenferna, A. 2020. Social tipping dynamics for stabilizing Earth's climate by 2050. *Proceedings of the National Academy of Sciences*, 117(5): 2354–2365.

Oxfam. 2018. Richest 1 percent bagged 82 percent of wealth created last year—poorest half of humanity got nothing. https://www.oxfam.org/en/press-releases/richest-1-percent-bagged-82-percent-wealth-created-last-year-poorest-half-humanity.

Parrique, T., Barth, J., Briens, F., Kerschner, C., Kraus-Polk, A., Kuokka-nen, A., and Spangenberg, J.H. 2019. Decoupling debunked: Evidence and arguments against green growth as a sole strategy for sustainability. *European Environmental Bureau. A study edited by the European Environment Bureau EEB*. Accessed August 10, 2020. https://eeb.org/library/decoupling-debunked/

Paulson, S. 2017. Degrowth: Culture, power and change. *Journal of Political Ecology*, 24(1): 425–448.

Perkins, P.E.E. 2019. Climate justice, commons, and degrowth. *Ecological Economics*, 160: 183–190.

Petersen, B., Stuart, D., and Gunderson, R. 2019. Reconceptualizing climate change denial: Ideological denialism misdiagnoses climate change and limits effective action. *Human Ecology Review*, 25(2): 117–141.

Polanyi, K. 2001 (1944). *The Great Transformation: The Political and Economic Origins of Our Time*. Boston, MA: Beacon Press.

Polimini, J.M., Myumi, K., Giampietro, M., and Alcott, B. 2008. *The Jevons Paradox and the Myth of Resource Efficiency Improvements*. London: Earthscan.

Pour, N., Webley, P.A., and Cook, P.J. 2017. A sustainability framework for bioenergy with carbon capture and storage (BECCS) technologies. *Energy Procedia*, 114: 6044–6056.

Pullinger, M. 2014. Working time reduction policy in a sustainable economy: Criteria and options for its design. *Ecological Economics*, 103: 11–19.

Rauch, E. 2000. What if, instead of using productivity increases to buy more possessions, we used them to get more time instead? http://groups.csail.mit.edu/mac/users/rauch/worktime/.

Reich, R.B. 2016. *Saving Capitalism: For the Many, Not the Few*. New York: Vintage.

Reid, W. V., Mooney, H. A., Cropper, A., Capistrano, D., Carpenter, S. R., Chopra, K., ... & Kasperson, R. (2005). *Ecosystems and human well-being-Synthesis: A report of the Millennium Ecosystem Assessment*. Island Press.

Reynolds, J.L., Parker, A., and Irvine, P. 2016. Five solar engineering tropes that have outstayed their welcome' *Earth's Future*, 4(12): 562–568.

Ripple, W.J., Wolf, C., Newsome, T.M., Barnard, P., and Moomaw, W.R. 2019. World scientists' warning of a climate emergency. *BioScience*, 70(1): 8–12.

Roberts, J.T., and Parks, B. 2006. *A Climate of Injustice: Global Inequality, North-South Politics, and Climate Policy*. Cambridge, MA: MIT Press.

Robertson, M.M. 2004. The neoliberalization of ecosystem services: Wetland mitigation banking and problems in environmental governance. *Geoforum*, 35(3), 361–373.

Robertson, M.M. 2006. The nature that capital can see: Science, state, and market in the commodification of ecosystem services. *Environment and Planning D: Society and Space*, 24(3), 367–387.

Robock, A. 2008a. Geoengineering: It's not a Panacea. *Geotimes,* 53(7): 58–58.

Robock, A. 2008b. 20 reasons why geoengineering may be a bad idea', *Bulletin of the Atomic Scientists,* 64(2): 14–18.

Robock, A., Marquardt, A., Kravitz, B., and Stenchikov, G. 2009. Benefits, risks, and costs of stratospheric geoengineering', *Geophysical Research Letters,* 36: 1–9.

Robock, A., Bunzl, M., Kravitz, B., and Stenchikov, G.L. 2010. A test for geoengineering? *Science,* 327(5965): 530–531.

Rockstrom, J., Steffen, W., Noone, K., Persson, A., Chapin, F.S., Lambin, E., Lenton, T.M., Scheffer, M., Folke, C., Schellnhuber, H.J., Nykvist, B., de Wit, C.A., Hughes, T., van der Leeuw, S., Rodhe, H., Sorlin, S., Snyder, P.K., Costanza, R., Svedin, U., Falkenmark, M., Karlberg, L., Corell, R.W., Fabry, V.J., Hansen, J., Walker, B., Liverman, D., Richardson, K., Crutzen, P., and Foley, J. 2009. Planetary boundaries: exploring the safe operating space for humanity. *Ecology and Society*, 14(2): 32. Accessed August 10, 2020. http://www.ecologyandsociety.org/vol14/iss2/art32/.

Rosenberg, K.V., Dokter, A.M., Blancher, P.J., Sauer, J.R., Smith, A.C., Smith, P.A., … Marra, P.P. 2019. Decline of the North American avifauna. *Science*, 366(6461): 120–124.

Rosnick, D. 2013. Recuced work hours as a means of slowing climate change. *Real-World Economic Review*, 63: 124–133.

Rosnick, D., and Weisbrot, M. 2006. *Are Shorter Working Hours Good for the Environment? A Comparison of U.S. and European Energy Consumption*. Washington, DC: Center for Economic and Policy Research.

Rudel, T.K., Schneider, L., Uriarte, M., Turner, B.L., DeFries, R., Lawrence, D., Geoghegan, J., Hecht, S., Ickowitz, A., Lambin, E.F., Birkenholtz, T., Baptista, S., and Grau, R. 2009. Agricultural intensification and changes in cultivated areas, 1970–2005. *Proceedings of the National Academy of Sciences of the United States of America*, 106(49): 20675–20680.

The Royal Society. 2009. *Geoengineering the Climate: Science, Governance and Uncertainty*. London: The Royal Society. Online. http://eprints.soton.ac.uk/156647/1/Geoengineering_the_climate.pdf?origin=publication_detail.

Santarius, T. 2012. *Green Growth Unravelled. How Rebound Effects Baffle Sustainability Targets When the Economy Keeps Growing*. Berlin: Wuppertal Institute.

Schmelzer, M. 2015. The growth paradigm: History, hegemony, and the contested making of economic growthmanship. *Ecological Economics*, 118: 262–271.

Schor, J. 2010. *Plenitude: The New Economics of True Wealth*. New York: Penguin Press.

Schor, J. 2015. Work-sharing. In *Degrowth: A Vocabulary for a New Era*, edited by G. D'Alisa, F. Demaria, and G. Kallis, 181–191. New York: Routledge.

Schor, J.B., and Jorgenson, A.K. 2019. Is it too late for growth? *Review of Radical Political Economics*, 51(2): 320–329.

Schmid, B. 2019. Degrowth and postcapitalism: Transformative geographies beyond accumulation and growth. *Geography Compass*, 13(11): 12470.

Schnaiberg, A. 1980. *The Environment: From Surplus to Scarcity*. Oxford: Oxford University Press.

Schroder, E., and Storm, S. 2018. Economic growth and carbon emissions: The road to 'hothouse earth' is paved with good intentions. Institute for New Economic Thinking, Working Paper 84.

Schweickart, D. 1992. Economic democracy—A worthy socialism that would really work. *Science & Society*, 56(1): 9–38.

Schweickart, D. 2016. Economic democracy: An ethically desirable socialism that is economically viable. The Next System Project Report. Retrieved from https://thenextsystem.org/economic-democracy.

Semuels, A. 2016. Does the economy really need to keep growing quite so much? The Atlantic. November 4. https://www.theatlantic.com/business/archive/2016/11/economic-growth/506423/.

Skandier, C. 2018. Quantitative Easing for the planet. https://thenextsystem.org/learn/stories/quantitative-easing-planet

Sol, J. 2019. Economics in the anthropocene: Species extinction or steady state economics. *Ecological Economics*, 165: 106392.

Sorrell, S. 2007. *The Rebound Effect: An Assessment of the Evidence for Economy-Wide Energy Savings from Improved Energy Efficiency*. London: UK Energy Research Centre.

Steffen, W., Richardson, K., Rockström, J., Cornell, S.E., Fetzer, I., Bennett, E.M., ... Folke, C. 2015. Planetary boundaries: Guiding human development on a changing planet. *Science*, 347(6223): 1259855.

Steffen, W., Rockstrom, J., Richardson, K., Lenton, T.M., Folke, C., Liverman, D., Summerhayes, C.P., Barnosky, A.D., Cornell, S.E., Crucifix, M., Donges, J.F., Fetzer, I., Lade, S.J., Scheffer, M., Winkelmann, R., and Schellnhuber, H.J. 2018. Trajectories of the earth system in the Anthropocene. *Proceedings of the National Academy of Sciences of the United States of America*, 115(33): 8252–8259.

Stiglitz, J.E. 2009. The great GDP swindle. *The Guardian*. September 12, 2009.

Stiglitz, J.E. 2019a. *Measuring What Counts: The Global Movement for Well-Being*. New York: The New Press.

Stiglitz, J.E. 2019b. It's time to retire metrics like GDP. They don't measure everything that matters. *The Guardian*. November 24. https://www.theguardian.

com/commentisfree/2019/nov/24/metrics-gdp-economic-performance-social-progress.

Stuart, D., Gunderson, R., and Petersen, B. 2019. Climate change and the Polanyian counter-movement: Carbon markets or degrowth? *New Political Economy*, 24(1): 89–102.

Stuart, D., Gunderson, R., and Petersen, B. 2020. Carbon geoengineering and the metabolic rift: Solution or social reproduction? *Critical Sociology*. Accessed August 10, 2020. https://doi.org/10.1177/0896920520905074.

Szasz, A. 2007. *Shopping Our Way to Safety: How We Changed from Protecting the Environment to Protecting Ourselves*. Minneapolis, MN: University of Minnesota Press.

The Next System Project. 2020. https://thenextsystem.org/

Thomas, C.D., Cameron, A., Green, R.E., Bakkenes, M., Beaumont, L.J., Collingham, Y.C., ... and Hughes, L. 2004. Extinction risk from climate change. *Nature*, 427(6970): 145.

Thorlakson, T., de Zegher, J.F., and Lambin, E.F. 2018. Companies' contribution to sustainability through global supply chains. *Proceedings of the National Academy of Sciences*, 115(9): 2072–2077.

Trainer, T. 2007. *Renewable Energy Cannot Sustain a Consumer Society*. New York: Springer.

Turner, P.A., Mach, K.J., Lobell, D.B., Benson, S.M., Baik, E., Sanchez, D.L., and Field, C.B. 2018. The global overlap of bioenergy and carbon sequestration potential. *Climatic Change*, 148(1–2): 1–10.

U.S. National Research Council. 2015a. *Climate Intervention: Carbon Dioxide Removal and Reliable Sequestration*. Committee on Geoengineering Climate: Technical Evaluation and Discussion of Impacts. Board on Atmospheric Sciences and Climate. Ocean Studies Board. Division on Earth and Life Studies. The National Academies Press. Online. http://www.nap.edu/openbook.php?record_id=18805.

U.S. National Research Council. 2015b. *Climate Intervention: Reflecting Sunlight to Cool Earth*. Committee on Geoengineering Climate: Technical Evaluation and Discussion of Impacts. Board on Atmospheric Sciences and Climate. Ocean Studies Board. Division on Earth and Life. The National Academies Press. Online. http://www.nap.edu/openbook.php?record_id=18988.

van Griethuysen, P. 2010. Why are we growth addicted? The hard way towards degrowth and the involutionary western development path. *Journal of Cleaner Production*, 18: 590–595.

Van Vuuren, D.P., Stehfest, E., Gernaat, D.E., Berg, M., Bijl, D.L., Boer, H.S., ... Hof, A.F. 2018. Alternative pathways to the 1.5°C target reduce the need for negative emission technologies. *Nature Climate Change*, 8: 391–397. https://doi.org/10.1038/s41558-018-0119-8.

van Zalk, J., and Behrens, P. 2018. The spatial extent of renewable and non-renewable power generation: A review and meta-analysis of power densities and their application in the US. *Energy Policy*, 123: 83–91.

Venette, S.J. 2003. *Risk Communication in a High Reliability Organization: APHIS PPQ's Inclusion of Risk in Decision Making.* Ann Arbor, MI: UMI Proquest Information and Learning.

Victor, P. 2010. Questioning economic growth. *Nature,* 468(7322): 370–371.

Victor, P. 2019. *Managing without Growth: Slower by Design, Not Disaster* (2nd ed.). Cheltenham: Edward Elgar Publishing.

Wallerstein, I. 1979. *The Capitalist World Economy.* New York: Cambridge University Press.

Wapner, P., and Willoughby, J. 2005. The irony of environmentalism: The ecological futility but political necessity of lifestyle change. *Ethics & International Affairs,* 19: 77–89.

Ward, J.D., Sutton, P.C., Werner, A.D., Costanza, R., Mohr, S.H., and Simmons, C.T. 2016. Is decoupling GDP growth from environmental impact possible? *PLoS One,* 11(10): e0164733.

Watts, N., Amann, M., Arnell, N., Ayeb-Karlsson, S., Belesova, K., Boykoff, M., ... Chambers, J. 2019. The 2019 report of the Lancet Countdown on health and climate change: Ensuring that the health of a child born today is not defined by a changing climate. *The Lancet,* 394(10211): 1836–1878.

Weis, T. 2010. The accelerating biophysical contradictions of industrial capitalist agriculture. *Journal of Agrarian Change,* 10(3): 315–341.

Werfel, S.H. 2017. Household behaviour crowds out support for climate change policy when sufficient progress is perceived. *Nature Climate Change,* 7: 512–515.

Wiedmann, T.O., Schandl, H., Lenzen, M., Moran, D., Suh, S., West, J., and Kanemoto, K. 2015. The material footprint of nations. *Proceedings of the National Academy of Sciences of the United States of America,* 112(20): 6271–6276.

Wright, E.O. 2010. *Envisioning Real Utopias.* London: Verso.

Wright, E.O. 2019. *How to be an Anti-Capitalist in the 21st Century.* London: Verso.

Wright, C., and Nyberg, D. 2015. *Climate Change, Capitalism, and Corporations.* Cambridge: Cambridge University Press.

York, R. 2010. The paradox at the heart of modernity: The carbon efficiency of the global economy. *International Journal of Sociology,* 40(2): 6–22.

York, R. 2012. Do alternative energy sources displace fossil fuels? *Nature Climate Change,* 2(6): 441–443.

York, R. 2016. Decarbonizing the energy supply may increase energy demand. *Sociology of Development,* 2(3): 265–272.

York, R., and Bell, S.E. 2019. Energy transitions or additions? Why a transition from fossil fuels requires more than the growth of renewable energy. *Energy Research & Social Science,* 51: 40–43.

York, R., Ergas, C., Rosa, E.A., and Dietz, T. 2011. It's a material world: Trends in material extraction in China, India, Indonesia, and Japan. *Nature and Culture,* 6(2): 103–122.

York, R., and McGee, J.A. 2016. Understanding the Jevons paradox. *Environmental Sociology*, 2(1): 77–87.

York, R., Rosa, E.A., and Dietz, T. 2009. A tale of contrasting trends: Three measures of the ecological footprint in China, India, Japan, and the United States, 1961–2003. *Journal of World-Systems Research*, 2: 134–146.

Zehner, O. 2012. *Green Illusions: The Dirty Secrets of Clean Energy and the Future of Environmentalism.* Lincoln: University of Nebraska Press.

Zhang, Z., Moore, J.C., Huisingh, D., and Yongzin, Z. 2015. Review of geo-engineering approaches to mitigating climate change. *Journal of Cleaner Production*, 103: 898–907.

Index

Note: *Italic* page numbers refer to figures and page numbers followed by "n" denote endnotes.